CLEP

College Level Examination Program

CLEP Five Favorites

XAMonline, Inc.
21 Orient Avenue
Melrose, MA 02176
Toll Free 1-800-301-4647
Email: info@xamonline.com
Web: www.xamonline.com
Fax: 1-617-583-5552

Library of Congress Cataloging-in-Publication Data

Wynne, Sharon

CLEP Five Favorites/ Sharon Wynne.
   ISBN: 978-1-60787-576-5

1. CLEP   2. Study Guides.

Disclaimer:
The opinions expressed in this publication are the sole works of XAMonline and were created independently from The College Board or other testing affiliates. Between the time of publication and printing, test standards as well as testing formats and website information may change that are not included in part or in whole within this product. XAMonline develops sample test questions, and they reflect similar content as on real tests; however, they are not former tests. XAMonline assembles content that aligns with test standards but makes no claims nor guarantees candidates a passing score. Numerical scores are determined by testing companies such as The College.

Cover photo provided by Production Perig/Shutterstock.com

Printed in the United States of America   œ-1
CLEP Five Favorites
ISBN: 978-1-60787-576-5

TABLE OF CONTENTS

I. The College-Level Examination Program

How the Program Works

CLEP exams are administered at over 1,800 institutions nationwide, and 2,900 colleges and universities award college credit to those who perform well on them. This rigorous program allows many self-directed students of a wide range of ages and backgrounds to demonstrate their mastery of introductory college-level material and pursue greater academic success. Students can earn credit for what they already know by getting qualifying scores on any of the 33 examinations.

The CLEP exams cover material that is taught in introductory-level courses at many colleges and universities. Faculty at individual colleges review the exams to ensure that they cover the important material currently taught in their courses.

Although CLEP is sponsored by the College Board, only colleges may grant credit toward a degree. To learn about a particular college's CLEP policy, contact the college directly. When you take a CLEP exam, you can request that a copy of your score report be sent to the college you are attending or planning to attend. After evaluating your score, the college will decide whether or not to award you credit for a certain course or courses, or to exempt you from them.

If the college decides to give you credit, it will record the number of credits on your permanent record, thereby indicating that you have completed work equivalent to a course in that subject. If the college decides to grant exemption without giving you credit for a course, you will be permitted to omit a course that would normally be required of you and to take a course of your choice instead.

The CLEP program has a long-standing policy that an exam may not be taken within the specified wait period. This waiting period provides you with an opportunity to spend additional time preparing for the exam or the option of taking a classroom course. If you violate the CLEP retest policy, the administration will be considered invalid, the score canceled, and any test fees will be forfeited. If you are a military service member, please note that DANTES will not fund retesting on a previously funded CLEP exam. However, you may personally fund a retest after the specified wait period.

The CLEP Examinations

CLEP exams cover material directly related to specific undergraduate courses taught during a student's first two years in college. The courses may be offered for three, four, six or eight semester hours in general areas such as mathematics, history, social sciences, English composition, natural sciences and humanities. Institutions will either grant credit for a specific course based on a satisfactory score on the related exam, or in the general area in which a satisfactory is earned. The credit is equal to the credit awarded to students who successfully complete the courses. See the Table of Contents for a complete list of all exam titles.

What the Examinations Are Like

CLEP exams are administered on computer and are approximately 90 minutes long, with the exception of College Composition, which is approximately 120 minutes long. Most questions are multiple-choice; other types of questions require you to fill in a numeric answer, to shade areas of an object, or to put items in the correct order. Questions using these kinds of skills are called zone, shade, grid, scale, fraction, numeric entry, histogram and order match questions.

CLEP College Composition includes a mandatory essay section, responses to which must be typed into the computer.

Some of the examinations have optional essays. You should check with the individual college or university where you are sending your score to see whether an optional essay is required for those exams. These essays are administered on paper and are scored by faculty at the institution that receives your score.

Where to Take the Examinations and How to Register

CLEP exams are administered throughout the year at over 1,800 test centers in the United States and select international sites. Once you have decided to take a CLEP examination, you can log into My Account at https://clepportal.collegeboard.org/myaccount to create and manage your own personal accounts, pay for CLEP exams and purchase study materials. You can self-register at any time by completing the online registration form.

Through My Account you can also access a list of institutions that administer CLEP and locate a test center in your area. **After paying for your exam through**

My Account, you must still contact the test center to schedule your CLEP exam.

If you are unable to locate a test center near you, call 800-257-9558 for more information.

ACE's College Credit Recommendation Service

The College Credit Recommendation Service (CREDIT) of the American Council on Education (ACE) enables you to put all of your educational achievements on a secure and universally accepted ACE transcript. All of your ACE-evaluated courses and examinations, including CLEP, appear in an easy-to-read format that includes ACE credit recommendations, descriptions and suggested transfer areas. The service is perfect for candidates who have acquired college credit at multiple ACE-evaluated organizations or credit-by-examination programs. You may have your transcript released at any time to the college of your choice. There is a one-time setup fee of $40 (includes the cost of your first transcript) and a fee of $15 for each transcript requested after release of the first. ACE has an additional transcript service for organizations offering continuing education units.

The College Credit Recommendation Service is offered through ACE's Center for Lifelong Learning. For more than 50 years, ACE has been at the forefront of the evaluation of education and training attained outside the classroom. For more information about ACE CREDIT, contact:

ACE CREDIT
One Dupont Circle, NW
Suite 250
Washington, DC 20036

ACE's Call Center is open Monday to Friday, 8:45 a.m. to 4:45 p.m., and can be reached at 866-205-6267 or CREDIT@ace.nche.edu. Staff are able to assist you with courses and certifications that carry ACE recommendations for both civilian organizations and training obtained through the military.

If you are already registered for an ACE transcript, you can access your records and order transcripts using the ACE Online Transcript System: https://www.acenet.edu/transcripts/.

ACE's Center for Lifelong Learning can be found on the Internet at: http://www.acenet.edu/ higher-education.

How Your Score Is Reported

You have the option of seeing your CLEP score immediately after you complete the exam, except in the case of College Composition, for which scores are available four to six weeks after the exam date. Once you choose to see your score, it will be sent automatically to the institution you have designated as a score recipient; it cannot be canceled. You will receive a candidate copy of your score before you leave the test center. If you have tested at the institution that you have designated as a score recipient, it will have immediate access to your test results.

If you do not want your score reported, you may select that as an option at the end of the examination *before the exam is scored*. Once you have selected the option to not view your score, the score is canceled.

The score will not be reported to the institution you have designated, and you will not receive a candidate copy of your score report. You will have to wait the specified wait period before you can take the exam again.

CLEP scores are kept on file for 20 years. During this period, for a small fee, you may have your transcript sent to another college or to anyone else you specify. Your score(s) will never be sent to anyone without your approval.

II. Approaching a College about CLEP

The following sections provide a step-by-step guide to learning about the CLEP policy at a particular college or university. The person or office that can best assist you may have a different title at each institution, but the following guidelines will lead you to information about CLEP at any institution.

Adults and other nontraditional students returning to college often benefit from special assistance when they approach a college. Opportunities for adults to return to formal learning in the classroom are now widespread, and colleges and universities have worked hard to make this a smooth process for older students. Many colleges have established special offices that are staffed with trained professionals who understand the kinds of problems facing adults returning to college. If you think you might benefit from such assistance, be sure to find out whether these services are available at your college.

How to Apply for College Credit

Step 1. *Obtain, or access online, the general information catalog and a copy of the CLEP policy from each college you are considering.*

Information about admission and CLEP policies can be obtained on the college's website at clep.collegeboard.org/search/colleges, or by contacting or visiting the admissions office. Ask for a copy of the publication in which the college's complete CLEP policy is explained. Also, get the name and the telephone number of the person to contact in case you have further questions about CLEP.

Step 2. If you have not already been admitted to a college that you are considering, look at its admission requirements for undergraduate students to see whether you qualify.

Whether you're applying for college admission as a high school student, transfer student or as an adult resuming a college career or going to college for the first time, you should be familiar with the requirements for admission at the schools you are considering. If you are a nontraditional student, be sure to check whether the school has separate admissions requirements that might apply to you. Some schools are very selective, while others are "open admission."

It might be helpful for you to contact the admissions office for an interview with a counselor. State why you want the interview and ask what documents you should bring with you or send in advance. (These materials may include a high school transcript, transcript of previous college work or completed application for admission.) Make an extra effort to have all the information requested in time for the interview.

During the interview, relax and be yourself. Be prepared to state honestly why you think you are ready and able to do college work. If you have already taken CLEP exams and scored high enough to earn credit, you have shown that you are able to do college work. Mention this achievement to the admissions counselor because it may increase your chances of being accepted. If you have not taken a CLEP exam, you can still improve your chances of being accepted by describing how your job training or independent study has helped prepare you for college-level work. Discuss with the counselor what you have learned from your work and personal experiences.

Step 3. *Evaluate the college's CLEP policy.*

Typically, a college lists all its academic policies, including CLEP policies, in its general catalog or on its website. You will probably find the CLEP policy statement under a heading such as Credit-by-Examination, Advanced Standing, Advanced Placement or External Degree Program. These sections can usually be found in the front of the catalog. You can also check out the institution's CLEP Policy by visiting clep.collegeboard.org/search/colleges.

Many colleges publish their credit-by-examination policies in separate brochures, which are distributed through the campus testing office, counseling center, admissions office or registrar's office. If you find a very general policy statement in the college catalog, seek clarification from one of these offices.

Review the material in the section of this chapter entitled "Questions to Ask about a College's CLEP Policy." Use these guidelines to evaluate the college's CLEP policy. If you have not yet taken a CLEP exam, this evaluation will help you decide which exams to take. Because individual colleges have different CLEP policies, a review of several policies may help you decide which college to attend.

Step 4. *If you have not yet applied for admission, do so as early as possible.*

Most colleges expect you to apply for admission several months before you enroll, and it is essential that you meet the published application deadlines. It takes time to process your application for admission. If you have yet to take a CLEP exam, you may want to take one or more CLEP exams while you are waiting for your application to be processed. Be sure to check the college's CLEP policy beforehand so that you are taking exams your college will accept for credit. You should also find out from the college when to submit your CLEP score(s).

Complete all forms and include all documents requested with your application(s) for admission.
Normally, an admission decision cannot be reached until all documents have been submitted and evaluated. Unless told to do so, do not send your CLEP score(s) until you have been officially admitted.

Step 5. *Arrange to take CLEP exam(s) or to submit your CLEP score(s).*

CLEP exams can be taken at any of the 1,800 test centers world-wide. To locate a test center near you. clep.collegeboard.org/search/test-centers. If you have already taken a CLEP exam, but did not have your score sent to your college, you can have an official transcript sent at any time for a small fee. Fill out the Transcript Request Form included on the same page as your exam score. If you do not have the form, visit clep.collegeboard.org/about/score to download a copy, or call 800-257-9558 to order a transcript using a major credit card. Completed forms should be faxed to 610-628-3726 or sent to the following address, along with a check or money order made payable to CLEP for $20 (this fee is subject to change).

CLEP Transcript Service
P.O. Box 6600
Princeton, NJ 08541-6600

Transcripts will only include CLEP scores for the past 20 years; scores more than 20 years old are not kept on file.

Your CLEP scores will be evaluated, probably by someone in the admissions office, and sent to the registrar's office to be posted on your permanent record once you are enrolled. Procedures vary from college to college, but the process usually begins in the admissions office.

Step 6. *Ask to receive a written notice of the credit you receive for your CLEP score(s).*

A written notice may save you problems later, when you submit your degree plan or file for graduation. In the event that there is a question about whether or not you earned CLEP credit, you will have an official record of what credit was awarded. You may also need this verification of course credit if you meet with an academic adviser before the credit is posted on your permanent record.

Step 7. *Before you register for courses, seek academic advising.*

A discussion with your academic adviser can help you to avoid taking unnecessary courses and can tell you specifically what your CLEP credit will mean to you. This step may be accomplished at the time you enroll. Most colleges have orientation sessions for new students prior to each enrollment period. During orientation, students are usually assigned academic advisers who then give them individual help in developing long-range plans and course schedules for the next semester. In conjunction with this counseling, you may be asked to take some additional tests so that you can be placed at the proper course level.

Questions to Ask about a College's CLEP Policy

Before taking CLEP exams for the purpose of earning college credit, try to find the answers to these questions:

1. *Which CLEP exams are accepted by the college?*

   A college may accept some CLEP exams for credit and not others — possibly not the exams you are considering. For this reason, it is important that you know the specific CLEP exams for which you can receive credit.

2. *Does the college require the optional free-response (essay) section for exams in composition and literature as well as the multiple-choice portion of the CLEP exam you are considering? Will you be required to pass a departmental test such as an essay, laboratory or oral exam in addition to the CLEP multiple-choice exam?*

   Knowing the answers to these questions ahead of time will permit you to schedule the optional free-response or departmental exam when you register to take your CLEP exam.

3. *Is CLEP credit granted for specific courses at the college? If so, which ones?*

   You are likely to find that credit is granted for specific courses and that the course titles are designated in the college's CLEP policy. It is not necessary, however, that credit be granted for a specific course for you to benefit from your CLEP credit. For instance, at many liberal arts colleges, all students must take certain types of courses; these courses may be labeled the core curriculum, general education requirements, distribution requirements or liberal arts requirements. The requirements are often expressed in terms of credit hours. For example, all students may be required to take at least six hours of humanities, six hours of English, three hours of mathematics, six hours of natural science and six hours of social science, with no particular courses in these disciplines specified. In these instances, CLEP credit may be given as "6 hrs. English Credit" or "3 hrs. Math Credit" without specifying for which English or mathematics courses credit has been awarded. To avoid possible disappointment, you should know before taking a CLEP exam what type of credit you can receive or whether you will be exempted from a required course but receive no credit.

4. *How much credit is granted for each exam you are considering, and does the college place a limit On the total amount of CLEP credit you can earn toward your degree?*

Not all colleges that grant CLEP credit award the same amount for individual exams. Furthermore, some colleges place a limit on the total amount of credit you can earn through CLEP or other exams. Other colleges may grant you exemption but no credit toward your degree. Knowing several colleges' policies concerning these issues may help you decide which college to attend. If you think you are capable of passing a number of CLEP exams, you may want to attend a college that will allow you to earn credit for all or most of them. Check out if your institution grants CLEP policy by visiting clep.collegeboard.org/search/colleges.

5. *What is the required score for earning CLEP credit for each exam you are considering?*

Most colleges publish the required scores for earning CLEP credit in their general catalogs or in brochures. The required score may vary from exam to exam, so find out the required score for each exam you are considering.

6. *What is the college's policy regarding prior course work in the subject in which you are considering taking a CLEP exam?*

Some colleges will not grant credit for a CLEP exam if the candidate has already attempted a college-level course closely aligned with that exam. For example, if you successfully completed English 101 or a comparable course on another campus, you will probably not be permitted to also receive CLEP credit in that subject. Some colleges will not permit you to earn CLEP credit for a course that you failed.

7. *Does the college make additional stipulations before credit will be granted?*

It is common practice for colleges to award CLEP credit only to their enrolled students. There are other stipulations, however, that vary from college to college. For example, does the college require you to formally apply for or to accept CLEP credit by completing and signing a form? Or does the college require you to "validate" your CLEP score by successfully completing a more advanced course in the subject? Getting answers to these and other questions will help to smooth the process of earning college credit through CLEP.

III. Preparing to Take CLEP Examinations

Test Preparation Tips

1. Familiarize yourself as much as possible with the test and the test situation before the day of the exam. It will be helpful for you to know ahead of time:

    a. how much time will be allowed for the test and whether there are timed subsections. (This information is included in the examination guides and in the CLEP Tutorial video.)

    b. what types of questions and directions appear on the exam. (See the examination guides.)

    c. how your test score will be computed.

    d. in which building and room the exam will be administered.

    e. the time of the test administration.

    f. direction, transit and parking information to the test center.

2. Register and pay your exam fee through My Account at https://clepportal.collegeboard.org/myaccount and print your registration ticket. Contact your preferred test center to schedule your appointment to test. Your test center may require an additional administration fee. Check with your test center and confirm the amount required and acceptable method of payment.

3. On the day of the exam, remember to do the following.

    a. Arrive early enough so that you can find a parking place, locate the test center, and get settled comfortably before testing begins.

    b. Bring the following with you:

        o   completed registration ticket
        o   any registration forms or printouts required by the test center. Make sure you have filled out all necessary paperwork in advance of your testing date.
        o   a form of valid and acceptable identification. Acceptable identification must:

X

- Be government-issued
- Be an original document — photocopied documents are not acceptable
- Be valid and current — expired documents (bearing expiration dates that have passed) are not acceptable, no matter how recently they may have expired
- Bear the test-taker's full name, in English language characters, exactly as it appears on the
- Registration Ticket, including the order of the names.
- Middle initials are optional and only need to match the first letter of the middle name when present on both the ticket and the identification.
- Bear a recent recognizable photograph that clearly matches the test-taker
- Include the test-taker's signature
- Be in good condition, with clearly legible text and a clearly visible photograph

Refer to the Exam Day Info page on the CLEP website (http://clep.collegeboard.org/exam-day-info) for more details on acceptable and unacceptable forms of identification.

- military test-takers, bring your Geneva Convention Identification Card. Refer to clep.collegeboard.org/military for additional information on IDs for active duty members, spouses, and civil service civilian employees.
- two number 2 pencils with good erasers. Mechanical pencils are prohibited in the testing room.

c. Leave all books, papers and notes outside the test center. You will not be permitted to use your own scratch paper; it will be provided by the test center.

d. Do not take a calculator to the exam. If a calculator is required, it will be built into the testing software and available to you on the computer. The CLEP Tutorial video will have a demonstration on how to use online calculators.

e. Do not bring a cell phone or other electronic devices into the testing room.

4. When you enter the test room:

   a. You will be assigned to a computer testing station. If you have special needs, be sure to communicate them to the test center administrator *before* the day you test.

   b. Be relaxed while you are taking the exam. Read directions carefully and listen to all instructions given by the test administrator. If you don't understand the directions, ask for help before the test begins. If you must ask a question that is not related to the exam after testing has begun, raise your hand and a proctor will assist you. The proctor cannot answer questions related to the exam.

   c. Know your rights as a test-taker. You can expect to be given the full working time allowed for taking the exam and a reasonably quiet and comfortable place in which to work. If a poor testing situation is preventing you from doing your best, ask whether the situation can be remedied. If it can't, ask the test administrator to report the problem on a Center Problem Report that will be submitted with your test results. You may also wish to immediately write a letter to CLEP, P.O. Box 6656, Princeton, NJ 08541- 6656. Describe the exact circumstances as completely as you can. Be sure to include the name of the test center, the test date and the name(s) of the exam(s) you took.

Accommodations for Students with Disabilities

If you have a disability, such as a learning or physical disability, that would prevent you from taking a CLEP exam under standard conditions, you may request accommodations at your preferred test center. Contact your preferred test center well in advance of the test date to make the necessary arrangements and to find out its deadline for submission of documentation and approval of accommodations. Each test center sets its own guidelines in terms of deadlines for submission of documentation and approval of accommodations.

Accommodations that can be arranged directly with test centers include:

- ZoomText (screen magnification)
- Modifiable screen colors
- Use of a reader, amanuensis, or sign language interpreter
- Extended time
- Untimed rest breaks

If the above accommodations do not meet your needs, contact CLEP Services at clep@info.collegeboard.org for information about other accommodations.

IV. Interpreting Your Scores

CLEP score requirements for awarding credit vary from institution to institution. The College Board, however, recommends that colleges refer to the standards set by the American Council on Education (ACE). All ACE recommendations are the result of careful and periodic review by evaluation teams made up of faculty who are subject-matter experts and technical experts in testing and measurement. To determine whether you are eligible for credit for your CLEP scores, you should refer to the policy of the college you will be attending. The policy will state the score that is required to earn credit at that institution. Many colleges award credit at the score levels recommended by ACE. However, some require scores that are higher or lower than these.

Your exam score will be printed for you at the test center immediately upon completion of the examination, unless you took College Composition. For this exam, you will receive your score four to six weeks after the exam date. Your CLEP exam scores are reported only to you, unless you ask to have them sent elsewhere. If you want your scores sent to a college, employer or certifying agency, you must select this option through My Account. This service is free only if you select your score recipient at the time you register to take your exam. A fee will be charged for each score recipient you select at a later date. Your scores are kept on file for 20 years. For a fee, you can request a transcript at a later date.

The pamphlet *What Your CLEP Score Means*, which you will receive with your exam score, gives detailed information about interpreting your scores. A copy of the pamphlet is in the appendix of this Guide. A brief explanation appears below.

How CLEP Scores Are Computed

In order to reach a total score on your exam, two calculations are performed.

First, your "raw score" is calculated. This is the number of questions you answer correctly. Your raw score is increased by one point for each question you answer correctly, and no points are gained or lost when you do not answer a question or answer it incorrectly.

Second, your raw score is converted into a "scaled score" by a statistical process called *equating*. Equating maintains the consistency of standards for test scores over time by adjusting for slight differences in difficulty between test forms. This ensures that your score does not depend on the specific test form you took or how well others did on the same form. Your raw score is converted to a scaled score that ranges from 20, the lowest, to 80, the highest. The final scaled score is the score that appears on your score report.

How Essays Are Scored

The College Board arranges for college English professors to score the essays written for the College Composition exam. These carefully selected college faculty members teach at two- and four-year institutions nationwide. The faculty members receive extensive training and thoroughly review the College Board scoring policies and procedures before grading the essays. Each essay is read and scored by two professors, the sum of the two scores for each essay is combined with the multiple-choice score, and the result is reported as a scaled score between 20 and 80. Although the format of the two sections is very different, both measure skills required for expository writing. Knowledge of formal grammar, sentence structure and organizational skills are necessary for the multiple-choice section, but the emphasis in the free-response section is on writing skills rather than grammar.

Optional essays for CLEP Composition Modular and the literature examinations are evaluated and scored by the colleges that require them, rather than by the College Board. If you take an optional essay, it will be sent to the institution you designate when you take the test. If you did not designate a score recipient institution when you took an optional essay, you may still select one as long as you notify CLEP within 18 months of taking the exam. Copies of essays are not held beyond 18 months or after they have been sent to an institution

Description of the Examination

The College Mathematics exam covers material generally taught in a college course for nonmathematics majors and majors in fields not requiring knowledge of advanced mathematics.

The examination contains approximately 60 questions to be answered in 90 minutes. Some of these are pretest questions that will not be scored. Any time test takers spend on tutorials and providing personal information is in addition to the actual testing time.

An online scientific (nongraphing) calculator will be available during the examination. Although a calculator is not necessary to answer most of the questions, there may be a few problems whose solutions are difficult to obtain without using a calculator. Since no calculator is allowed during the examination except for the online calculator provided, is it recommended that prior to the examination you become familiar with the use of the online calculator.

For more information about downloading the practice version of the scientific (nongraphing) calculator, please visit the College Mathematics description on the CLEP website, **clep.collegeboard.org**

It is assumed that test takes are familiar with currently taught mathematics vocabulary, symbols, and notation.

Knowledge and Skills Required

Questions on the College Mathematics examination require test takers to demonstrate the following abilities in the approximate proportion indicated.

- Solving routine, straightforward problems (about 50% of the examination)
- Solving nonroutine problems requiring an understanding of concepts and the application of skills and concepts (about 50% of the examination)

The subject matter of the College Mathematics examination is drawn from the following topics. The percentages next to the main topics indicate the approximate percentage of exam questions on that topic.

1

20% **Algebra**
- Solving equations, linear inequalities, and systems of linear equations by analytical and graphical methods
- Interpretation, representation, and evaluation of functions: numerical, graphical, symbolic, and descriptive methods
- Graphs of functions: translations, horizontal and vertical reflections, and symmetry about the x-axis, the y-axis, and the origin
- Linear and exponential growth
- Applications

10% **Counting and Probability**
- Counting problems: the multiplication rule, combinations and permutations
- Probability: union, intersection, independent events, mutually exclusive events, complementary events, conditional probabilities, and expected value
- Applications

15% **Data Analysis and Statistics**
- Data interpretation and representation: tables, bar graphs, line graphs, circle graphs, pie charts, scatterplots, and histograms
- Numerical summaries of data: mean (average), median, mode, and range
- Standard deviation, normal distribution (conceptual questions only)
- Applications

20% **Financial Mathematics**
- Percents, percent change, markups, discounts, taxes, profit, and loss
- Interest: simple, compound, continuous interest, effective interest rate, effective annual yield or annual percentage rate (APR)
- Present value and future value
- Applications

10% Geometry
- Properties of triangles and quadrilaterals: perimeter, area, similarity, and the Pythagorean theorem
- Parallel and perpendicular lines
- Properties of circles: circumference, area, central angles, inscribed angles, and sectors
- Applications

15% Logic and Sets
- Logical operations and statements: conditional statements, conjunctions, disjunctions, negations, hypotheses, logical conclusions, converses, inverses, counterexamples, contrapositives, logical equivalence
- Set relationships, subsets, disjoint sets, equality of sets, and Venn diagrams
- Operations on sets: union, intersection, complement, and Cartesian product
- Applications

10% Numbers
- Properties of numbers and their operations: integers and rational, irrational, and real numbers (including recognizing rational and irrational numbers)
- Elementary number theory: factors and divisibility, primes and composites, odd and even integers, and the fundamental theorem of arithmetic
- Measurement: unit conversion, scientific notation, and numerical precision
- Absolute value
- Applications

SAMPLE TEST

DIRECTIONS: Read each item and select the best response.

1. Which of the following is closed under division?

    I. $\left\{\dfrac{1}{3}, 1, 3\right\}$

    II. $\{-1, 1\}$
    III. $\{-1, 0, 1\}$

    A. I only

    B. II only

    C. III only

    D. I and II

    E. II and III

2. Which of the following is always composite if x is an odd positive integer and y is an even positive integer greater than 1 ?

    A. $x+y$

    B. $|x+y|$

    C. $x+2y$

    D. $3x+y$

    E. $3xy$

3. Find the LCM of 25, 18, and 24.

    A. 1200

    B. 1800

    C. 2400

    D. 3600

    E. 10,800

4. Solve for x:
    $|3x|+6=21$

    A. [9, -5]

    B. [-9, 5]

    C. [-5, 0, 5]

    D. [-5, 5]

    E. [-9, 9]

5. Which graph represents the solution set for $x^2 - 5x > -6$?

A.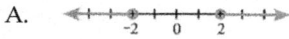

B.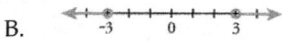

C.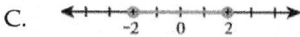

D.

E.

6. What is the equation of the graph shown below?

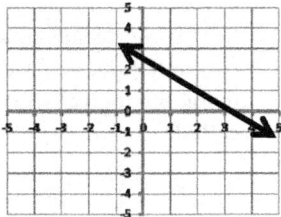

A. $x + 2y = 4$

B. $x - 2y = 4$

C. $2x + y = 4$

D. $x + 2y = -4$

E. $x - 2y = -4$

7. Solve the following inequality: $-2x > 4$

A. $x > -2$

B. $x < -2$

C. $x > 2$

D. $x > -8$

E. $x < 2$

8. Which equation represents a circle centered on the origin with radius 3?

A. $x^2 + y^2 = 3$

B. $x^2 + y^2 = 6$

C. $x^2 + y^2 = 9$

D. $x^2 + y^2 = 36$

E. $x^2 - y^2 = 9$

9. Given that D is a distance, M is a mass, T is a time, and V is a velocity, which of the following units could be used to measure $\frac{MTV}{D}$?

   A. feet

   B. meters

   C. grams

   D. seconds

   E. miles per hour

10. **Cubic meters are used to measure which of the following?**

    A. Distance

    B. Length

    C. Area

    D. Volume

    E. Mass

11. What figure best describes a data set in which many items are clustered near the median value with a smaller number of values less than or greater than the median at greater distances on each side?

    A. A parabola

    B. A normal curve

    C. A line of best fit

    D. A Cartesian curve

    E. A Newtonian curve

12. **If you prove a theorem by showing that an attempt to prove the opposite of the theorem leads to a contradiction, you are using the logical strategy called:**

    A. Inductive reasoning

    B. Exhaustive proof

    C. Proof by attraction

    D. Direct proof

    E. Indirect proof

13. Compute the area of the shaded region, given a radius of 7 meters. Point O is the center.

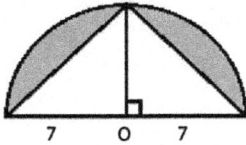

7   O   7

A. 14.0

B. 28.0

C. 55.9

D. 104.9

E. 153.9

14. A garden measures 25 by 40m including a circular fishpond with radius 3m. What is the area of the garden not including the fishpond?

A. 101.7 m²

B. 111.2 m²

C. 971.7 m²

D. 981.2 m²

E. 990.6 m²

15. The base of cone A has 3 times as great an area as the base of cone B, but the height of cone A is only $\frac{1}{3}$ the height of cone B. Which statement is true?

A. Cone A has 9 times the volume of cone B.

B. Cone A has 3 times the volume of cone B.

C. Cone A and cone B have the same volume.

D. Cone B has 3 times the volume of cone A.

E. Cone B has 9 times the volume of cone A.

16. Find the area of the figure depicted below.

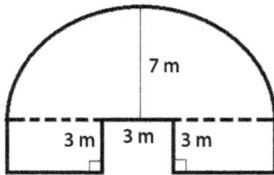

7 m

3 m 3 m 3 m

A. 109.9 m^2

B. 118.9 m^2

C. 142.9 m^2

D. 144.9 m^2

E. 186.9 m^2

17. State the domain of the function $f(x) = \dfrac{2x-14}{x^2-9}$.

A. $x \neq 3$

B. $x \neq 3, 7$

C. $x \neq 3, -3$

D. $x \neq 7$

E. $x = 3, -3, 7$

18. Which of the following is a factor of the expression $6x^2 - 5x - 14$?

A. $3x + 7$

B. $6x + 7$

C. $6x - 7$

D. $6x - 5$

E. $x + 2$

19. Solve for x by factoring: $x^2 + x - 6 = 0$

A. $x = (-3, 2)$

B. $x = (3, -2)$

C. $x = (-6, 1)$

D. $x = (6, -1)$

E. no real solutions

20. Which of the following is equivalent to $\sqrt[b]{x^a}$?

A. $x^{\frac{a}{b}}$

B. $x^{\frac{b}{a}}$

C. $a^{\frac{x}{b}}$

D. $b^{\frac{x}{a}}$

E. $a^{\frac{b}{x}}$

21. Given $f(x) = 2x + 1$ and $g(x) = x^2 - 1$, determine $g(f(x))$.

A. $4x^2 + 4x - 1$

B. $4x^2 + 4x + 1$

C. $4x^2$

D. $4x^2 - 1$

E. $4x^2 + 4x$

22. Compute the median for the following data set: $\{9, 11, 18, 13, 12, 21\}$

A. 12

B. 12.5

C. 13

D. 14

E. 15.5

23. Which graph represents the equation?

$$y = x^2 + 3x ?$$

A.

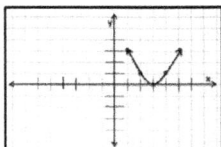

B.

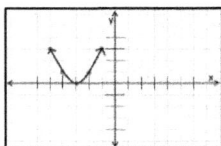

C.

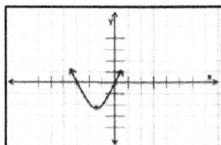

D.

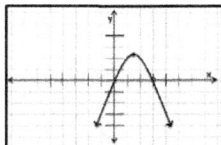

E.

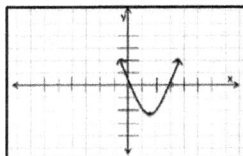

24. What would be the best measure of central tendency for the following collection of high temperatures on 10 successive days?

{27, 24, 33, 24, 36, 65, 34, 30, 28, 29}

A. Mean

B. Either mean or median

C. Median

D. Mode

E. Either median or mode

25. If the correlation between two variables is zero, the association between the two variables is

A. Negative linear

B. Positive linear

C. Quadratic

D. Direct variation

E. Random

26. Which of the following is not a valid method of collecting statistical data?

A. Random sampling

B. Systematic sampling

C. Volunteer response

D. Weighted sampling

E. Cylindrical sampling

27. A jar contains 3 red marbles and 7 green ones. What is the probability that a marble picked at random from the jar will be red?

A. $\dfrac{1}{3}$

B. $\dfrac{1}{7}$

C. $\dfrac{3}{7}$

D. $\dfrac{3}{10}$

E. $\dfrac{7}{10}$

28. A die is rolled several times. What is the probability that a 6 will not appear before the fourth roll of the die?

A. $\dfrac{125}{216}$

B. $\dfrac{625}{1296}$

C. $\dfrac{1}{2}$

D. $\dfrac{5}{6}$

E. $\dfrac{1}{216}$

29. There is a 30% chance of rain this Saturday and a 30% chance of rain on Sunday as well. What is the chance of rain on both days?

A. 9%

B. 30%

C. 49%

D. 60%

E. 70%

30. Which equation matches the data in the table?

x	3	4	5	6
y	7	8	9	10

A. $y = 2x - 1$

B. $y = 2x + 1$

C. $y = -x + 10$

D. $y = x + 4$

E. $y = x - 4$

31. Which table could be generated by the equation?
$y = x^2 + 2x - 1$?

A.

x	1	2	3	4
y	2	5	8	11

B.

x	1	2	3	4
y	4	9	16	25

C.

x	1	2	3	4
y	1	5	11	19

D.

x	1	2	3	4
y	2	7	13	21

E.

x	1	2	3	4
y	2	7	14	23

32. The fees charged by a parking garage are as follows:

Hours	1	2	3	4	5
Fee	$12	$19	$26	$33	$40

How would you summarize the fees charged?

A. $12 an hour

B. $5 plus $7 per hour

C. $15 an hour with a $3 discount

D. $4 plus $8 per hour

E. $3 plus $9 per hour

33. Which of the following is a solution to
$x^2 + 4x + 4 = 25$?

A. 2

B. -2

C. -7

D. -3

E. 5

34. Solve the following system of equations:

$$2x + y = 8$$
$$4x + 2y = 20$$

A. $x = 2, y = 4$

B. $x = 3, y = 1$

C. $x = 4, y = 0$

D. no solutions

E. an infinite number of solutions

35. If an initial deposit of $10,000 is made to a savings account with interest compounded continuously at an annual rate of 6% how much money is in the account after 5 years?

A. $13,498.59

B. $3,498.56

C. $13,382.26

D. $3,382.26

E. $13,000.00

36. A dance team comes prepared with a tango, a waltz, a disco number, a salsa routine, and a ballet selection. In how many different orders can they present their routines?

A. 5

B. 25

C. 120

D. 625

E. 3125

37. You can choose 3 selections from a buffet table with 8 dishes. How many different plates can you choose?

A. 6

B. 24

C. 56

D. 336

E. 6561

38. Leah has 4 blouses, 3 skirts, and 6 pairs of shoes. How many different outfits can she dress herself in?

A. 12

B. 13

C. 24

D. 72

E. 720

39. Hiroshi surveys his classmates to find what percent of them come to school on the bus, by car, by subway, by bicycle, or on foot. What is the best way to display his results?

A. A line graph

B. A box plot

C. A stem-and-leaf plot

D. A scatterplot

E. A circle graph

40. Which equation could be used as a line of best fit for the scatterplot below?

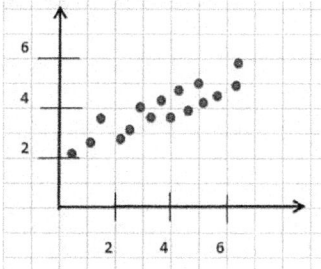

A. $y = \dfrac{1}{2}x + 2$

B. $y = 2x + 2$

C. $y = -2x + 2$

D. $y = \dfrac{1}{2}x - 2$

E. $y = \dfrac{1}{2}x + 2$

41. To find the standard variation of a data set, you first compute the square of the distance of each data item from the mean of all the data items. Then what do you do?

A. Add all the squared distances and take the square root of the result.

B. Find the mean of the squared distances and take the square root of the result.

C. Multiply the squared distances and take the nth root of the result.

D. Multiply the square root of the sum of the squared distances by the mean of the squared distances.

E. Multiply the sum of the squared distances by the square root of the mean of the squared distances.

42. In which data set is the mode greater than the median?

    A. {9,11,11,12,14}

    B. {13,15,17,19,21}

    C. {8,11,12,12,19}

    D. {9,9,9,14,20}

    E. {7,11,13,14,14}

43. Of the 200 students in the junior class, 8% are in the Spanish Club. How many juniors are in the Spanish Club?

    A. 4

    B. 8

    C. 16

    D. 20

    E. 25

44. When Olga bought a boat for $1750 she paid an excise tax of $78.75. What was the percent of the tax?

    A. 4.5%

    B. 5.5%

    C. 6.3%

    D. 7%

    E. 7.5%

45. A bank account pays 5% interest yearly. How large an amount would have to be deposited to earn $75 interest in a year?

    A. $375

    B. $875

    C. $1200

    D. $1500

    E. $3750

46. A stock previously trading at $96 a share is now trading at $88 a share. What is the percent of change in the value of the stock?

A. -8%

B. -8.3%

C. -12%

D. -12.5%

E. -16%

47. The admission price to tour the Haunted House has been changed from $25 to $30. What is the percent of change in the admission price?

A. 5%

B. 16.7%

C. 20%

D. 25%

E. 30%

48. Eileen's Bakery had expenses of $62,5000 last year and sales of $68,750. What was the profit as a percent of the expenses?

A. 6.25%

B. 10%

C. 12%

D. 15%

E. 16.7%

49. Tim's Typewriters had expenses of $26,200 last year and sales of $19,912. What was the loss as a percent of the expenses?

A. 7%

B. 8%

C. 16.7%

D. 20%

E. 24%

50. A stock that had been selling at $30 a share increased its share price by 20% Later in the day the same stock suffered a 20% decrease in its share price. What was the price at the end of the day?

A. $24

B. $28.80

C. $30

D. $33

E. $36

51. A sweater is marked "25% off." The sale price is $36. What was the price before the discount?

A. $27

B. $32

C. $40

D. $45

E. $48

52. The sum of $1440 is deposited in a bank which pays 6% simple interest per year. After how many years will there be $1872 in the account?

A. 2.5 years

B. 3 years

C. 4 years

D. 5 years

E. 8 years

53. A bank pays 5% interest on deposits, compounded yearly. If $14,000 is deposited, how much will be in the account 3 years later?

A. $14,350

B. $15,435

C. $16,100

D. $16,206.75

E. $17,500

54. Which statement is logically equivalent to the following: If it's raining, my roof is leaking.

  A. If my roof isn't leaking, it isn't raining.

  B. If my roof is leaking, it's raining.

  C. If it isn't raining, my roof isn't leaking.

  D. If my roof is leaking, it's not raining

  E. If it's raining, my roof isn't leaking.

55. What is the union of set A and set B?

  Set A: {2,4,5,9,11}
  Set B: {3,5,8,11,13}

  A. {2, 3, 4, 5, 5, 8, 9, 11, 11, 13}

  B. {2, 3, 4, 5, 8, 9, 11, 13}

  C. {5, 11}

  D. {2, 3, 4, 8, 9, 13}

  E. {5, 9, 13, 20, 24}

56. What is the intersection of set A and set B?

  Set A: {1,3,7,9,10,12,14}
  Set B: {1,4,7,8,11,12,15}

  A. {1, 1, 3, 4, 7, 7, 8, 9, 10, 11, 12, 12, 14, 15}

  B. {1, 3, 4, 7, 8, 9, 10, 11, 12, 14, 15}

  C. {1, 7, 12}

  D. {1, 1, 7, 7, 12, 12}

  E. {3, 4, 8, 9, 10, 11, 14, 15}

57. Which statement is NOT implied by the Venn diagram below?

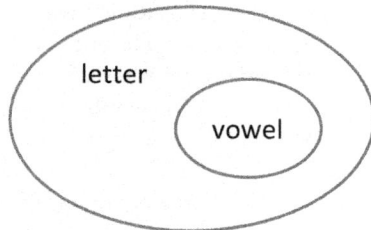

  A. No vowels are not letters.

  B. All vowels are letters.

  C. Some letters are vowels.

  D. Some letters are not vowels.

  E. Some vowels are not letters.

58. A total of 150 students have signed up for musical activities. There are 82 students in the choir and 80 students in the band. How many students are in both the band and the choir?

   A. 12

   B. 24

   C. 42

   D. 70

   E. 162

59. Chris's older brother Mike is 2 years younger than Florence. When Tom's younger sister Rhoda was 8, Chris was 3 Florence is not older than Rhoda. Name the five people in ascending order of age.

   A. Tom, Rhoda, Florence, Mike, Chris

   B. Tom, Florence, Rhoda, Mike, Chris

   C. Chris, Mike, Florence, Rhoda, Tom

   D. Chris, Mike, Rhoda, Florence, Tom

   E. Chris, Rhoda, Mike, Florence, Tom

60. Disprove the following statement by offering a counterexample: "Multiplying two numbers together produces a larger number than either of the two original numbers."

   A. $\sqrt{2} \times \sqrt{2}$

   B. 1.25×1.78

   C. -3×-3

   D. 0.5×0.6

   E. -0.8×-0.3

ANSWER KEY

Question Number	Correct Answer	Your Answer	Question Number	Correct Answer	Your Answer
1	B		31	E	
2	E		32	B	
3	B		33	C	
4	D		34	D	
5	E		35	A	
6	A		36	C	
7	B		37	C	
8	C		38	D	
9	C		39	E	
10	D		40	A	
11	B		41	B	
12	E		42	E	
13	B		43	C	
14	C		44	A	
15	C		45	D	
16	A		46	B	
17	C		47	C	
18	B		48	B	
19	A		49	E	
20	A		50	B	
21	E		51	E	
22	B		52	D	
23	C		53	D	
24	C		54	A	
25	E		55	B	
26	E		56	C	
27	D		57	E	
28	A		58	A	
29	A		59	C	
30	D		60	D	

RATIONALES

1. Which of the following is closed under division?

    I. $\left\{\dfrac{1}{3},1,3\right\}$

    II. $\{-1,1\}$

    III. $\{-1,0,1\}$

    A. I only

    B. II only

    C. III only

    D. I and II

    E. II and III

The answer is B

Set I is not closed under division, because $\dfrac{1}{3}$ divided by 3 is $\dfrac{1}{9}$, a number outside the set. Set III is not closed under division, because it is not possible to divide either –1 or 1 by 0.

2. Which of the following is always composite if x is an odd positive integer and y is an even positive integer greater than 1 ?

    A. $x + y$

    B. $|x + y|$

    C. $x + 2y$

    D. $3x + y$

    E. $3xy$

The answer is E

$3xy$ must be composite, since 3, x, and y are all factors.

3. **Find the LCM of 25, 18, and 24.**

 A. 1,200

 B. 1,800

 C. 2,400

 D. 3,600

 E. 10,800

The answer is B
The LCM must contain 2 factors of 5 to be a multiple of 25. It must contain 2 factors of 3 and a factor of 2 to be a multiple of 18. And it must contain 3 factors of 2 and a factor of 3 to be a multiple of 24. Therefore, the LCM must contain the following factors: 5×5×3×3×2×2×2= 1800

4. **Solve for x :**
 $$|3x|+6=21$$

 A. [9, -5]

 B. [-9, 5]

 C. [-5, 0, 5]

 D. [-5, 5]

 E. [-9, 9]

The answer is D
Write two equations to express the two possibilities:

$$3x+6=21$$
$$-3x+6=21$$

Solving the two equations gives 5 and –5.

5. **Which graph represents the solution set for $x^2 - 5x > -6$?**

A.

B.

C.

D.

E.

The answer is E

Gathering all terms on the left gives $x^2 - 5x + 6 > 0$. Replace the inequality symbol with an equals sign and solve for x: $x = 2$, and $x = 3$. A graph of the parabola makes clear that it is greater than 0 for x-values less than 2 or greater than 3 or greater, but less than 0 when $2 \le x \le 3$.

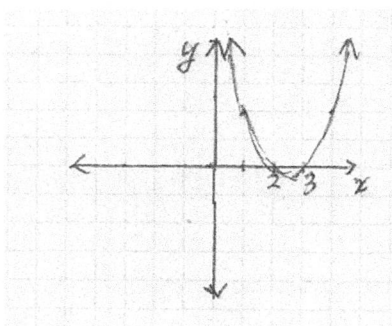

6.   What is the equation of the graph shown below?

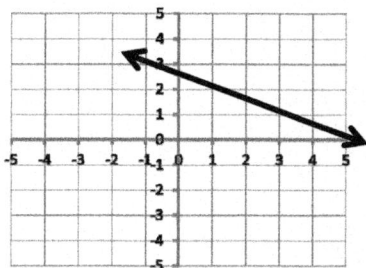

A. $x + 2y = 4$

B. $x - 2y = 4$

C. $2x + y = 4$

D. $x + 2y = -4$

E. $x - 2y = -4$

The answer is A

Replacing x with 0 gives a y-intercept of 2. Replacing y with 0 gives an x-intercept of 4. The equation is linear, so a line can be drawn between the two points to complete the graph.

7.   Solve the following inequality: $-2x > 4$

A. $x > -2$

B. $x < -2$

C. $x > 2$

D. $x > -8$

E. $x < 2$

The answer is B

To solve for x, you must divide by –2, but dividing by a negative number reverses the inequality, so the result is $x < -2$.

8. Which equation represents a circle centered on the origin with radius 3?

   A. $x^2 + y^2 = 3$

   B. $x^2 + y^2 = 6$

   C. $x^2 + y^2 = 9$

   D. $x^2 + y^2 = 36$

   E. $x^2 - y^2 = 9$

The answer is C
The equation for a circle centered on the origin is $x^2 + y^2 = r^2$. Since $r = 3$, the equation in this case is $x^2 + y^2 = 9$.

9. Given that D is a distance, M is a mass, T is a time, and V is a velocity, which of the following units could be used to measure $\frac{MTV}{D}$?

   A. feet

   B. meters

   C. grams

   D. seconds

   E. miles per hour

The answer is C
Try some sample units and see how they interact:
Let the distance be in miles, the mass be in grams, the time be in hours, and the velocity in miles per hour. Then the units to express $\frac{MTV}{D}$ would be

$g \times h \times \frac{mi}{h} \times \frac{1}{mi}$ Hours and miles cancel out, leaving only grams.

10.   Cubic meters are used to measure which of the following?

A.   Distance

B.   Length

C.   Area

D.   Volume

E.   Mass

The answer is D
Distance and length are measured in linear meters. Area is measured in square meters. Mass is not measured in meters of any kind. Of the choices, only volume is measured in cubic meters.

11.   What figure best describes a data set in which many items are clustered near the median value with a smaller number of values less than or greater than the median at greater distances on each side?

A.   A parabola

B.   A normal curve

C.   A line of best fit

D.   A Cartesian curve

E.   A Newtonian curve

The answer is B
The figure described is a normal curve, called normal because data from the natural world tend to present a shape in which median values are commoner than extreme ones.

12. If you prove a theorem by showing that an attempt to prove the opposite of the theorem leads to a contradiction, you are using the logical strategy called:

    A. Inductive reasoning

    B. Exhaustive proof

    C. Proof by attraction

    D. Direct proof

    E. Indirect proof

The answer is E
Such a proof is called "indirect" because it uses the opposite of the theorem instead of the theorem itself.

13. Compute the area of the shaded region, given a radius of 7 meters. Point O is the center.

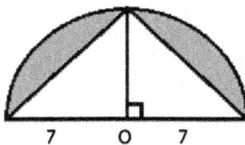

    A. 14.0

    B. 28.0

    C. 55.9

    D. 104.9

    E. 153.9

The answer is B
The area of the half circle is $\frac{49\pi}{2}$ The two triangles are equivalent to a square
7 meters on a side. So the shaded area $= \frac{49\pi}{2} - 49 \approx 28.0.$

14. A garden measures 25m by 40m including a circular fishpond with radius 3m. What is the area of the garden not including the fishpond?

   A. 101.7 m²

   B. 111.2 m²

   C. 971.7 m²

   D. 981.2 m²

   E. 990.6 m²

The answer is C

The area of the garden is $25 \times 40 = 1000$ m². The area of the fishpond is $3^2 \pi \approx 28.3$ m². The difference is about 971.7 m².

15.   The base of cone A has 3 times as great an area as the base of cone B, but the height of cone A is only $\frac{1}{3}$ the height of cone B.

Which statement is true?

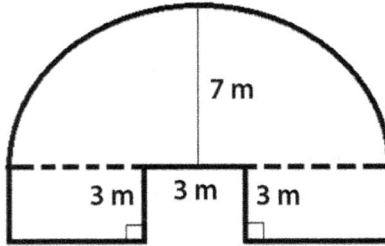

A.   Cone A has 9 times the volume of cone B.

B.   Cone A has 3 times the volume of cone B

C.   Cone A and cone B have the same volume.

D.   Cone B has 3 times the volume of cone A.

E.   Cone B has 9 times the volume of cone A.

The answer is C

Let h be the height of cone B and let b be the area of the base of cone B. Using the formula for the volume of a cone, the volume of cone B is $\frac{1}{3}bh.$. The base of cone $A = 3b$, while the height of cone $A = \frac{h}{3}$. Therefore, the volume of cone A is $\frac{1}{3}(3b)\left(\frac{h}{3}\right) = \frac{1}{3}bh,$ the same as cone B.

COLLEGE MATHEMATICS

16.   Find the area of the figure depicted below.

   A.   109.9 m²

   B.   118.9 m²

   C.   142.9 m²

   D.   144.9 m²

   E.   186.9 m²

The answer is A
The area of the circle is $\frac{49\pi}{2}$. The dotted line equals a diameter, twice the
length of the radius, or 14. Subtracting the gap of 3 m, the two rectangles add
up to a length of 11 m times a width of 3 m. So the total area is
$\frac{49\pi}{2} + 33 \approx 109.9 \text{ m}^2.$

17.   State the domain of the function $f(x) = \frac{2x - 14}{x^2 - 9}.$

   A. $x \neq 3$

   B. $x \neq 3, 7$

   C. $x \neq 3, -3$

   D. $x \neq 7$

   E. $x = 3, -3, 7$

The answer is C
The domain must exclude values of x that would cause the denominator of
the function to equal 0. Therefore, both –3 and 3 are excluded from the
domain.

31

18. Which of the following is a factor of the expression $6x^2 - 5x - 14$?

    A. $3x + 7$

    B. $6x + 7$

    C. $6x - 7$

    D. $6x - 5$

    E. $x + 2$

The answer is B

To factor the expression, multiply 6 times 14 to get 84. Then look for two factors of 84 that differ by 5: 7 and 12. Use these factors to rewrite the middle term as $7x - 12x$. You can then factor the expression as $(6x + 7)(x - 2)$.

19. Solve for x by factoring: $x^2 + x - 6 = 0$

    A. $x = (-3, 2)$

    B. $x = (3, -2)$

    C. $x = (-6, 1)$

    D. $x = (6, -1)$

    E. no real solutions

The answer is A

Factoring the left side of the equation gives us $(x + 3)(x - 2) = 0$. Setting each factor equal to 0 gives us solutions of –3 and 2.

20.   Which of the following is equivalent to $\sqrt[b]{x^a}$?

A. $x^{\frac{a}{b}}$

B. $x^{\frac{b}{a}}$

C. $a^{\frac{x}{b}}$

D. $b^{\frac{x}{a}}$

E. $a^{\frac{b}{x}}$

The answer is A
Taking the bth root of x^a is equivalent to dividing the exponent of x^a by b.

21.   Given $f(x)=2x+1$ and $g(x)=x^2-1$, determine $g(f(x))$.

A. $4x^2 + 4x - 1$

B. $4x^2 + 4x + 1$

C. $4x^2$

D. $4x^2 - 1$

E. $4x^2 + 4x$

The answer is E
If $f(x)=2x+1$, $g(f(x))=(2x+1)^2-1=4x^2-4x.$

22. Compute the median for the following data set: {9, 11, 18, 13, 12, 21}

    A. 12

    B. 12.5

    C. 13

    D. 14

    E. 15.5

The answer is B

In ascending order, the set is {9, 11, 12, 13, 18, 21}

Since there are an even number of data items, the median is halfway between the two most central items when the items are put in ascending order, in this case the third and fourth.

23. **Which graph represents the equation?**

$$y = x^2 + 3x?$$

A.

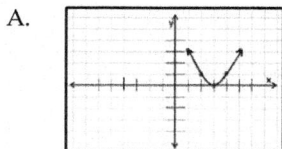

B.

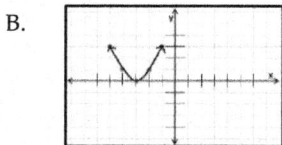

C.

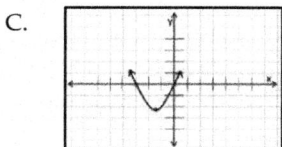

D.

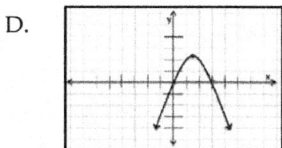

E.

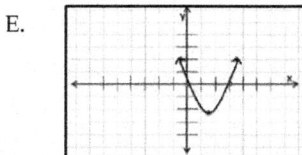

The answer is C

Since $x^2 + 3x$ can be factored as $x(x + 3)$, the function has zeroes at 0 and –3.

Since the first term is positive, the parabola opens up. Choice C fits these specifications.

24. What would be the best measure of central tendency for the following collection of high temperatures on 10 successive days?

$$\{27, 24, 33, 24, 36, 65, 34, 30, 28, 29\}$$

A. Mean

B. Either mean or median

C. Median

D. Mode

E. Either median or mode

The answer is C
Since the data contains an outlier, the mean would be skewed too high. The mode is the smallest data item and therefore also not a good representation. The median is the best available representation of the data as a whole.

25. If the correlation between two variables is zero, the association between the two variables is

A. Negative linear

B. Positive linear

C. Quadratic

D. Direct variation

E. Random

The answer is E
Choices A, B, C, and D all describe some form of correlation between the two variables. Only a random association shows zero correlation.

26.   **Which of the following is not a valid method of collecting statistical data?**

   A.   Random sampling

   B.   Systematic sampling

   C.   Volunteer response

   D.   Weighted sampling

   E.   Cylindrical sampling

The answer is E
Choices A, B, C, D describe methods of data collection with varying degrees of potential usefulness and prohibition. There is no such thing as cylindrical sampling.

27.   **A jar contains 3 red marbles and 7 green ones. What is the probability that a marble picked at random from the jar will be red?**

   A. $\dfrac{1}{3}$

   B. $\dfrac{1}{7}$

   C. $\dfrac{3}{7}$

   D. $\dfrac{3}{10}$

   E. $\dfrac{7}{10}$

The answer is D
Three marbles are red out of a total of 10 marbles, yielding a probability of 3/10.

28. A die is rolled several times. What is the probability that a 6 will not appear before the fourth roll of the die?

  A. $\dfrac{125}{216}$

  B. $\dfrac{625}{1296}$

  C. $\dfrac{1}{2}$

  D. $\dfrac{5}{6}$

  E. $\dfrac{1}{216}$

The answer is A

Each time the die is rolled, the chance of rolling a number other than 6 is $\dfrac{5}{6}$.

The probability that this will happen three times is $\dfrac{5}{6} \times \dfrac{5}{6} \times \dfrac{5}{6} = \dfrac{125}{216}$.

29.   There is a 30% chance of rain this Saturday and a 30% chance of rain on Sunday as well. What is the chance of rain on both days?

A.   9%

B.   30%

C.   49%

D.   60%

E.   70%

The answer is A
The probability of two things both happening is the product of the two probabilities: 0.3(0.3) = 0.09 = 9%.

30.   Which equation matches the data in the table?

x	3	4	5	6
y	7	8	9	10

A. $y=2x-1$

B. $y=2x+1$

C. $y=-x+10$

D. $y=x+4$

E. $y=x-4$

The answer is D
Each y-value is 4 greater than the corresponding x-value.

31.   Which table could be generated by the equation?

$$y = x^2 + 2x - 1?$$

A.

x	1	2	3	4
y	2	5	8	11

B.

x	1	2	3	4
y	4	9	16	25

C.

x	1	2	3	4
y	1	5	11	19

D.

x	1	2	3	4
y	2	7	14	23

E.

x	1	2	3	4
y	2	7	13	21

The answer is E

Substitute <u>each</u> x-value into the equation and see if the result matches the y-value. Only in table E do all the y-values correspond to the values found by substituting the x-values into the equation.

32.   The fees charged by a parking garage are as follows:

Hours	1	2	3	4	5
Fee	$12	$19	$26	$33	$40

How would you summarize the fees charged?

A. $12 an hour

B. $5 plus $7 per hour

C. $15 an hour with a $3 discount

D. $4 plus $8 per hour

E. $3 plus $9 per hour

The answer is B
Each additional hour costs $7 more, so the rate must be $7 an hour, which leaves $5 as the initial fee.

33.   Which of the following is a solution to $x^2 + 4x + 4 = 25$?

A.   2

B.   -2

C.   -7

D.   -3

E.   5

The answer is C
Taking the square root of both sides yields $x + 2 = \pm 5$.
Therefore, $x = 3$ or -7.

34.   Solve the following system of equations:

$$2x + y = 8$$
$$4x + 2y = 20$$

A. $x = 2, y = 4$

B. $x = 3, y = 1$

C. $x = 4, y = 0$

D.   no solutions

E.   an infinite number of solutions

The answer is D
Multiply the first equation by 2 and subtract from the second equation. The result is 0 = 4. A system of equations that resolves to an untrue statement has no solutions.

35.   If an initial deposit of $10,000 is made to a savings account with interest compounded continuously at an annual rate of 6% how much money is in the account after 5 years?

A, $13,498.59

B. $3498.59

C. $13,382.26

D. $3,382.26

E. $13,000.00

The answer is A
Continuously compounded interest is calculated using the formula Pe^{rt}, where P is the amount of the principal, r is the annual rate, and t is the time in years. $10,000 \times e^{0.06 \times 5} = 10,000e^{0.3} \approx 13,498.59$.

36.   A dance team comes prepared with a tango, a waltz, a disco number, a salsa routine, and a ballet selection. In how many different orders can they present their routines?

   A.   5

   B.   25

   C.   120

   D.   625

   E.   3125

The answer is C
Any of the 5 routines could be the first number. The second number could be any of the remaining 4, the third could be any of the remaining 3, and so on. The total number of choices is $5 \times 4 \times 3 \times 2 \times 1 = 120$.

37.   You can choose 3 selections from a buffet table with 8 dishes. How many different plates can you choose?

   A.   6

   B.   24

   C.   56

   D.   336

   E.   6561

The answer is C
Since the order of items on your plate does not matter, it is combinations rather than permutations we need to find. The number of combinations of k items out of n possible selections is given by the formula

$$\frac{n!}{(n-k)!k!}. \quad \frac{8!}{5!3!} = 56$$

38.   Leah has 4 blouses, 3 skirts, and 6 pairs of shoes. How many different outfits can she dress herself in?

    A. 12

    B. 13

    C. 24

    D. 72

    E. 720

The answer is D
By the Fundamental Counting Principle, the number of different outfits is $4 \times 3 \times 6 = 72$.

39.   Hiroshi surveys his classmates to find what percent of them come to school on the bus, by car, by subway, by bicycle, or on foot. What is the best way to display his results?

    A. A line graph

    B. A box plot

    C. A stem-and-leaf plot

    D. A scatterplot

    E. A circle graph

The answer is E
A circle graph is the best way to display what portion of the whole data set is occupied by each item.

40.   Which equation could be used as a line of best fit for the scatterplot below?

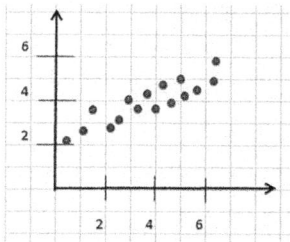

A. $y = \dfrac{1}{2}x + 2$

B. $y = 2x + 2$

C. $y = -2x + 2$

D. $y = \dfrac{1}{2}x - 2$

E. $y = 2x - 2$

The answer is A

The data appear to start around 2, and the y-values are generally rising less fast than the x-values, so the slope appears to be less than 1. $\dfrac{1}{2}x + 2$ is the best fit among the choices.

41. To find the standard variation of a data set, you first compute the square of the distance of each data item from the mean of all the data items. Then what do you do?

    A. Add all the squared distances and take the square root of the result.

    B. Find the mean of the squared distances and take the square root of the result.

    C. Multiply the squared distances and take the nth root of the result.

    D. Multiply the square root of the sum of the squared distances by the mean of the squared distances.

    E. Multiply the sum of the squared distances by the square root of the mean of the squared distances.

The answer is B
Choice B correctly completes the process of finding a standard variation.

42. In which data set is the mode greater than the median?

    A. {9, 11, 11, 12, 14}

    B. {13, 15, 17, 19, 21}

    C. {8, 11, 12, 12, 19}

    D. {9, 9, 9, 14, 20}

    E. {7, 11, 13, 14, 14}

The answer is E
In choice E, the median is 13 and the mode 14.

43. Of the 200 students in the junior class, 8% are in the Spanish Club. How many juniors are in the Spanish Club?

    A. 4

    B. 8

    C. 16

    D. 20

    E. 25

The answer is C

The number of juniors in the Spanish club is 8 % of 200 or 16.

44. When Olga bought a boat for $1,750.00 she paid an excise tax of $78.75. What was the percent of the tax?

    A. 4.5%

    B. 5.5%

    C. 6.3%

    D. 7%

    E. 7.5%

The answer is A

To find the percent of tax, divide the tax by the sales price and multiply by 100. $\frac{78.75}{1750} \times 100 = 4.5$, so the tax rate is 4.5%.

45.   A bank account pays 5% interest yearly. How large an amount would have to be deposited to earn $75 interest in a year?

A. $375

B. $875

C. $1200

D. $1500

E. $3750

The answer is D
If a principal of x dollars earns $75 at 5% interest, then $0.5x = 75$. Multiplying both sides by 20 yields $x = 1500$, so the amount of the principal must be $1500.

46.   A stock previously trading at $96 a share is now trading at $88 a share. What is the percent of change in the value of the stock?

A. -8%

B. -8.3%

C. -12%

D. -12.5%

E. -16%

The answer is B
The percent of change is found by dividing the amount of the change by the original value, then multiplying by 100. The change is –$8, and the original amount is $96. $\frac{-8}{96} \times 100 \approx -8.3$, So the stock price has changed about –8.3%.

47.   The admission price to tour the Haunted House has been changed from $25 to $30. What is the percent of change in the admission price?

   A.   5%

   B.   16.7%

   C.   20%

   D.   25%

   E.   30%

The answer is C
The amount of change is +$5, and the original value is $25. $\frac{5}{25} = \frac{1}{5} = 20\%$.

48.   Eileen's Bakery had expenses of $62,500 last year and sales of $68,750. What was the profit as a percent of the expenses?

   A.   6.25%

   B.   10%

   C.   12%

   D.   15%

   E.   16.7%

The answer is B
The amount of change is $6,250. $\frac{6250}{62500} = \frac{1}{10} = 10\%$.

49. Tim's Typewriters had expenses of $26,200 last year and sales of $19,912. What was the loss as a percent of the expenses?

    A. 7%

    B. 8%

    C. 16.7%

    D. 20%

    E. 24%

The answer is E
The amount of loss was $6288, and 6288/26200 = 24%.

50. A stock that had been selling at $30 a share increased its share price by 20%. Later in the day the same stock suffered a 20% decrease in its share price. What was the price at the end of the day?

    A. $24

    B. $28.80

    C. $30

    D. $33

    E. $36

The answer is B
After the $30 price increased by 20%, it was $36.

51. A sweater is marked "25% off." The sale price is $36. What was the price before the discount?

    A. $27

    B. $32

    C. $40

    D. $45

    E. $48

The answer is E
If the original price has been decreased by 25%, the sale price is 75% of the original. Solving $36 = 0.75x$ yields $x = 48$.

52. The sum of $1440 is deposited in a bank which pays 6% simple interest per year. After how many years will there be $1872 in the account?

    A. 2.5 years

    B. 3 years

    C. 4 years

    D. 5 years

    E. 8 years

The answer is D
After each year is completed, the amount in the account is increased by $0.06(1440) = \$86.40$ dollars. The number of years required to bring the account to $1872 is $\dfrac{1872-1440}{86.40} = \dfrac{432}{86.40} = 5$

53.   A bank pays 5% interest on deposits, compounded yearly. If $14,000 is deposited, how much will be in the account 3 years later?

   A. $14,350

   B. $15,435

   C. $16,100

   D. $16,206.75

   E. $17,500

The answer is D
The amount in the account after 3 years will be $14,000 \times 1.05^3 = \$16.206.75$.

54.   Which statement is logically equivalent to the following: If it's raining, my roof is leaking.

   A.   If my roof isn't leaking, it isn't raining.

   B.   If my roof is leaking, it's raining.

   C.   If it isn't raining, my roof isn't leaking.

   D.   If my roof is leaking, it's not raining

   E.   If it's raining, my roof isn't leaking.

The answer is A
The contrapositive of a true statement is also true. In this case, rain always makes my roof leak, so the absence of a leak could only be explained by the absence of rain.

55.   **What is the union of set A and set B?**

>   Set A: {2,4,5,9,11}
>   Set B: {3,5,8,11,13}

A.   {2,3,4,5,5,8,9,11,11,13}

B.   {2,3,4,5,8,9,11,13}

C.   {5,11}

D.   {2,3,4,8,9,13}

E.   {5,9,13,20,24}

The answer is B
The union of the two sets contains every number that is in either set.
Numbers that are in both sets are included only once in the union set.

56.   **What is the intersection of set A and set B?**

>   Set A: {1,3,7,9,10,12,14}
>   Set B: {1,4,7,8,11,12,15}

A.   {1,1,3,4,7,7,8,9,10,11,12,12,14,15}

B.   {1,3,4,7,8,9,10,11,12,14,15}

C.   {1,7,12}

D.   {1,1,7,7,12,12}

E.   {3,4,8,9,10,11,14,15}

The answer is C
The intersection of the two sets contains only those numbers that are in both
sets.

57.   Which statement is NOT implied by the Venn diagram below?

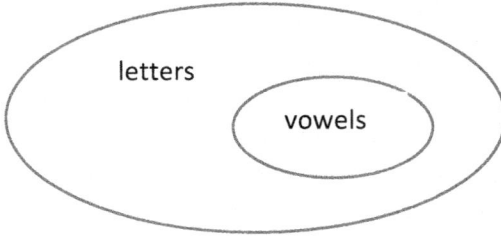

    A.   No vowels are not letters.

    B.   All vowels are letters.

    C.   Some letters are vowels.

    D.   Some letters are not vowels.

    E.   Some vowels are not letters.

The answer is E

The diagram shows that the class of vowels is totally included in the class of letters, so there are no vowels that are not letters.

58. A total of 150 students have signed up for musical activities. There are 82 students in the choir and 80 students in the band. How many students are in both the band and the choir?

    A. 12

    B. 24

    C. 42

    D. 70

    E. 162

The answer is A
The sum of 82 choir members and 80 band members is 162, but only 150 students are involved. The explanation is that 12 students are in both the band and choir, and are therefore counted twice when the two memberships are added.

59. Chris's older brother Mike is 2 years younger than Florence. When Tom's younger sister Rhoda was 8, Chris was 3 Florence is younger than Rhoda. Name the five people in ascending order of age.

    A. Tom, Rhoda, Florence, Mike, Chris

    B. Tom, Florence, Rhoda, Mike, Chris

    C. Chris, Mike, Florence, Rhoda, Tom

    D. Chris, Mike, Rhoda, Florence, Tom

    E. Chris, Rhoda, Mike, Florence, Tom

The answer is C
Statement 1 allows as to put Chris, Mike, and Florence in ascending order. The second statement allows us to put Rhoda and Tom in ascending order. Since Florence is younger than Rhoda, both Rhoda and Tom are older than Chris, Mike, and Florence, allowing us to put all five in ascending order.

60. Disprove the following statement by offering a counterexample: "Multiplying two numbers together produces a larger number than either of the two original numbers."

A. $\sqrt{2} \times \sqrt{2}$

B. 1.25×1.78

C. -3×-3

D. 0.5×0.6

E. -0.8×-0.3

The answer is D

The product of 0.5 and 0.6 is 0.3, which is smaller than either of the two original numbers. The other multiplications produce a product larger than either of the numbers multiplied.

Description of the Examination

The College Algebra examination covers material that is usually taught in a one-semester college course in algebra. Nearly half of the test is made up of routine problems requiring basic algebraic skills; the remainder involves solving nonroutine problems in which candidates must demonstrate their understanding of concepts. The test includes questions on basic algebraic operations; linear and quadratic equations, inequalities and graphs; algebraic, exponential and logarithmic functions; and miscellaneous other topics. It is assumed that candidates are familiar with currently taught algebraic vocabulary, symbols and notation. The test places little emphasis on arithmetic calculations. However, an online scientific calculator (nongraphing) will be available during the examination.

The examination contains approximately 60 questions to be answered in 90 minutes. Some of these are pretest questions that will not be scored. Any time candidates spend on tutorials and providing personal information is in addition to the actual testing time.

Knowledge and Skills Required

Questions on the College Algebra examination require candidates to demonstrate the following abilities in the approximate proportions indicated.

- Solving routine, straightforward problems (about 50% of the examination)
- Solving nonroutine problems requiring an understanding of concepts and the applications of skills and concepts (about 50% of the examination)

The subject matter of the College Algebra examination is drawn from the following topics. The percentages next to the main topics indicate the approximate percentage of exam questions on that topic.

25%   **Algebraic Operations**

- Operations with exponents
- Factoring and expanding polynomials
- Operations with algebraic expressions
- Absolute value
- Properties of logarithms

25%   **Equations and Inequalities**

- Linear equations and inequalities
- Quadratic equations and inequalities
- Absolute value equations and inequalities
- Systems of equations and inequalities
- Exponential and logarithmic equations

30%   **Functions and Their Properties**

- Definition, interpretation and representation/modeling (graphical, numerical, symbolic, verbal)
- Domain and range

- Evaluation of functions
- Algebra of functions
- Graphs and their properties (including intercepts, symmetry, transformations)
- Inverse functions

20%   **Number Systems and Operations**

- Real numbers
- Complex numbers
- Sequences and series
- Factorials and Binomial Theorem

SAMPLE TEST

DIRECTIONS: Read each item and select the best response

1. **Which of the following is a factor of the expression** $9x^2 + 6x - 35$?

    A. $3x - 5$

    B. $3x - 7$

    C. $x + 3$

    D. $x - 2$

    E. $x - 3$

2. **Given** $f(x) = 3x - 2$ **and** $g(x) = x^2$, **determine** $g(f(x))$.

    A. $3x^2 - 2$

    B. $9x^2 + 4$

    C. $9x^2 - 12x + 4$

    D. $3x^3 - 2$

    E. $9x^2 - 36$

3. **Solve for** x: $18 = 4 + |2x|$

    A. $\{-11, 7\}$

    B. $\{-7, 0, 7\}$

    C. $\{-7, 7\}$

    D. $\{-11, 11\}$

    E. $\{-8, 8\}$

4. **Solve for** x **by factoring:** $2x^2 - 3x - 2 = 0$

    A. $x = (-1, 2)$

    B. $x = (0.5, -2)$

    C. $x = (-0.5, 2)$

    D. $x = (1, -2)$

    E. $x = (-2, 2)$

5. Which of the following illustrates an inverse property?

   A. $a+b=a-b$

   B. $a+b=b+a$

   C. $a+0=a$

   D. $a+(-a)=0$

   E. $b-a=0$

6. The conjugate of $4+5i$ is

   A. $-4+5i$

   B. $4-5i$

   C. $4i+5$

   D. $4i-5$

   E. $-4-5i$

7. Simplify:
   $(6+3i)-(4-2i)$

   A. $2+5i$

   B. $2+i$

   C. $10+5i$

   D. $2-2i$

   E. $10-5i$

8. Simplify:
   $$\frac{10}{1+3i}$$

   A. $-1.25(1-3i)$

   B. $1.25(1+3i)$

   C. $1+3i$

   D. $1-3i$

   E. $10+3i$

9. Solve
   $(2b^3 \cdot b^2)^3$

   A. $3b^9$

   B. $2b^8$

   C. $8b^{15}$

   D. $2b^{18}$

   E. $8b^{18}$

10. Which of the following is incorrect?

   A. $\left(x^2 y^3\right)^2 = x^4 y^6$

   B. $m^2 (2n)^3 = 8m^2 n^3$

   C. $\dfrac{m^3 n^4}{m^2 n^2} = mn^2$

   D. $\left(x + y^2\right)^2 = x^2 + y^4$

   E. $\left(2s^{-4} w^4\right)\left(7sw^{-5}\right) = \dfrac{14}{s^3 w}$

11. Evaluate $3^{\frac{1}{2}}\left(9^{\frac{1}{3}}\right)$

   A. $27^{\frac{5}{6}}$

   B. $9^{\frac{7}{12}}$

   C. $3^{\frac{5}{6}}$

   D. $3^{\frac{6}{7}}$

   E. $9^{\frac{12}{7}}$

12. Simplify:
$$\frac{4x^0 y^{-2} z^3}{4x}$$

   A. $\dfrac{z^3}{y^2}$

   B. $\dfrac{z^3}{y^2 x}$

   C. $\dfrac{z^2}{y^3}$

   D. $\dfrac{z^3}{x^2 y}$

   E. $z^3 y^2$

13. The exponential equation $2^5 = 32$ can be written as:

   A. $\log_2 (5) = 32$

   B. $\log_{10} (32) = 5$

   C. $\log_5 (32) = 2$

   D. $\log_2 (32) = 5$

   E. $\log_5 (2) = 32$

14. Which equation corresponds to the logarithmic statement $\log_x k = m$?

    A. $x^m = k$

    B. $k^m = x$

    C. $x^k = m$

    D. $m^x = k$

    E. $k^x = m$

15. Solve for x:
    $\log_6(x-5) + \log_6 x = 2$

    A. $x = 9$

    B. $x = 2, x = 7$

    C. $x = 6$

    D. $x = -2, x = -7$

    E. $x = -4, x = -9$

16. Solve for the slope m and y -intercept:
    $3x + 2y = 14$

    A. $m = \frac{2}{3}, y = 5$

    B. $m = -\frac{3}{2}, y = 7$

    C. $m = \frac{3}{2}, y = -7$

    D. $m = -\frac{2}{3}, y = -5$

    E. $m = 2, y = 7$

17. Simplify:
    $-4(-4x-1) - 4(7x+3)$

    A. $-44x + 16$

    B. $12x - 16$

    C. $44x - 16$

    D. $-12x - 8$

    E. $-11x + 2$

18. **Solve** $-2x < 5$.

   A. $x < -\dfrac{5}{2}$

   B. $x > -\dfrac{2}{5}$

   C. $x > -\dfrac{5}{2}$

   D. $x > \dfrac{5}{2}$

   E. $x < \dfrac{5}{2}$

19. **Solve** $10 \le 3x + 4 \le 19$.

   A. $2 \le x \le 5$

   B. $-2 \le x \le 5$

   C. $x \le 5$

   D. $x \ge 2$

   E. $-5 \le x \le -2$

20. **Solve for** x:
$$x^2 + 10x - 24 = 0$$

   A.   (-5, 12)

   B.   (-10, 8)

   C.   (12, 2)

   D.   (10, 8)

   E.   (-12, 2)

21. **Find a quadratic equation with roots of 4 and -9.**

   A. $x^2 - 5x + 36 = 0$

   B. $x^2 + 5x - 36 = 0$

   C. $4x^2 - 9x - 5 = 0$

   D. $x^2 + 4x - 9 = 0$

   E. $5x^2 - 9x + 4 = 0$

22. **Solve:**
$$4800 \le 200x - 2x^2$$

   A. $-40 \le x \le 40$

   B. $x \le 40$

   C. $40 \le x \le 60$

   D. $x = 40$

   E. $x = -40$

23. **Solve:**
$|3x+2|=4x+5$

    A. $x=-3$

    B. $x=-1$

    C. $x=3$

    D. $x=1$

    E. $x=6$

24. **Solve:**
$|3x-5|=\dfrac{1}{2}$

    A. $x=-\dfrac{11}{6},-\dfrac{3}{2}$

    B. $x=-\dfrac{11}{6},\dfrac{3}{2}$

    C. $x=\dfrac{11}{6},-\dfrac{3}{2}$

    D. $x=\dfrac{11}{6},\dfrac{3}{2}$

    E. $x=11,\dfrac{3}{2}$

25. **Solve:**
$2|3x+9|<36$

    A. $x<-9$

    B. $x>3$

    C. $3<x<9$

    D. $-9<x<-3$

    E. $-9<x<3$

26. **Solve for x and y:**
$$4x+3y=-1$$
$$5x+4y=1$$

    A. $x=-7, y=9$

    B. $x=7, y=-9$

    C. $x=7, y=9$

    D. $x=-7, y=-9$

    E. $x=y=7$

27. **Which point is in the solution set for the system of inequalities below?**

    $x - 7 > 1$
    $y < 2x - 1$

    A. $(-1, -1)$

    B. $(-2, -1)$

    C. $(0, 1)$

    D. $(0, -2)$

    E. $(1, 1)$

28. **Solve:**
    $3^{2x-1} = 27$

    A. $x = 2$

    B. $x = -3$

    C. $x = -2$

    D. $x = 3$

    E. $x = \dfrac{2}{3}$

29. **Solve:** $\log_b(x^2) = \log_b(2x - 1)$

    A. $x = -2$

    B. $x = 1$

    C. $x = -1$

    D. $x = 2$

    E. $x = 4$

30. **Solve:**
    $\log_2(x) + \log_2(x - 2) = 3$

    A. x = 4

    B. x = -4, 2

    C. x = -4, -2

    D. x = 4, -2

    E. x = 2

31. **If** $f(x) = -3x + 8$, **find**
    $f(5)$.

    A. 23

    B. -23

    C. 7

    D. -7

    E. 21

32. Find the zeros of the function
$$h(x) = \frac{x-9}{x+2}.$$

A. $\{9\}$

B. $\{-2\}$

C. $\left\{-\dfrac{9}{2}\right\}$

D. $\{-2, 9\}$

E. This function has no zeros.

33. Which number line shows the solution to
$7x - 5 \geq 9x - 17$?

A.

B.

C.

D.

E.

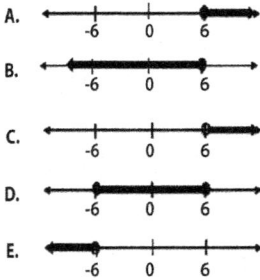

34. Which graph represents the equation of $y = x^2 + 3x$?

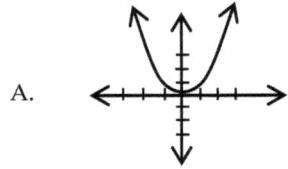

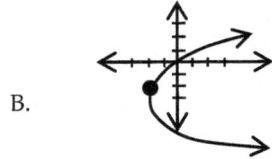

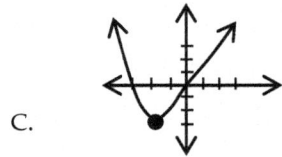

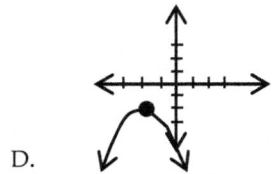

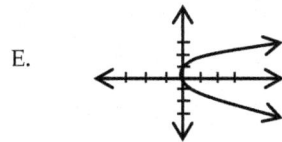

A.

B.

C.

D.

E.

35. Based on the given table, if $y_1 = x^3$, what is the equation for y_2?

x	-2	-1	0	1	2	3
y_1	-8	-1	0	1	8	27
y_2	-18	-11	-10	-9	-2	-17

A. $y_2 = x^5$

B. $y_2 = -x^3$

C. $y_2 = (-x)^3$

D. $y_2 = (x-10)^3$

E. $y_2 = x^3 - 10$

36. Identify the domain and range of the relation:
$\{(2,-5),(4,31),(11,-11),(-21,3)\}$

A. Domain is { -21 } range is { -11 }

B. Domain is {-5, 31, -11, 3}, range is {2, 4, 11, -21}.

C. Domain is {11} and range is {31}

D. Domain and range are indeterminate.

E. Domain is {2, 4, 11, -21}, range is {-5, 31, -11, 3}.

37. Determine the domain of $y = -\sqrt{-2x+3}$.

A. $x = 3$

B. $x \le \dfrac{3}{2}$

C. $x > \dfrac{3}{2}$

D. $x = 2$

E. $x = 0$

38. For the function $h(x)$ whose graph is shown below, select the domain and range.

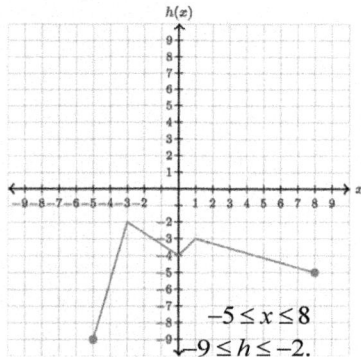

$-5 \le x \le 8$
$-9 \le h \le -2$.

A. Domain is , range is

B. Domain is -5, range is -5.
$-5 \le x \le 8,$

C. Range is $-9 \le h \le 2$. domain is $x \ge -5,$

D. Domain is $h \ge -9$. range is

E. Domain is 8, range is -2.

39. **Given** $f(x) = 3x^2 - 7x + 5$, **find** $f(-4)$.

   A. -71

   B. 25

   C. 81

   D. -25

   E. 71

40. **For** $h(x) = 3x^2 + ax - 1$, $h(3) = 8$, **find the value of** a.

   A. 6

   B. -6

   C. -18

   D. 18

   E. 27

41. **Given** $f(x) = 3x^2 - 7x + 5$, **find** $\dfrac{f(x+h) - f(x)}{h}$

   A. $7h$

   B. $6xh - 7$

   C. $6x + 3h - 7$

   D. $3x + 6h + 7$

   E. $5x$

42. **Find the** x- **and** y-**intercepts for** $5x - 3y = 15$.

   A. $x = 0, y = 0$

   B. $x = -3, y = 5$

   C. $x = -1, y = 5$

   D. $x = -5, y = 3$

   E. $x = 3, y = -5$

43. **Which of the figures is a reflection of the triangle shown?**

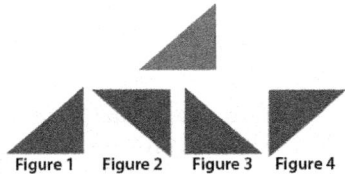

Figure 1   Figure 2   Figure 3   Figure 4

   A. Figure 1 and Figure 4

   B. Figure 4 and Figure 3

   C. Figure 2 and Figure 1

   D. Figures 2, 3 and 4

   E. Figure 1 and Figure 2

44. Name the transformation shown.

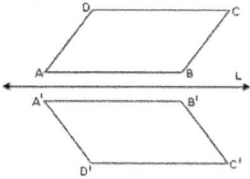

A. Translation

B. Rotation

C. Reflection

D. Dilation

E. Cannot be determined

45. Find the inverse of
$y = 3x - 2$.

A. $y = \dfrac{1}{3x - 2}$

B. $y = \dfrac{x + 2}{3}$

C. $x = \dfrac{y + 2}{3}$

D. $y - 3x - 2 = 0$

E. $3x - y - 2 = 0$

46. Find the inverse of
$f(x) = -\dfrac{1}{3}x + 1$

A. $f^{-1}(x) = 1$

B. $f^{-1}(x) = 3x$

C. $f^{-1}(x) = 3x - 3$

D. $f^{-1}(x) = -3x + 3$

E. $f^{-1}(x) = x^2$

47. If $f(x) = 3x - 2$ and
$g(x) = \dfrac{x}{3} + \dfrac{2}{3}$, which of the
following is true:

A. $f(x)$ is the inverse of $g(x)$.

B. $f(x) = g^{-1}(x)$

C. There is no connection between $f(x)$ and $g(x)$.

D. $g(x) = f(x)$

E. A and B

69

48. **Identify the real numbers in the list:** $1.67, \pi, \sqrt{5}, 0$

    A. All

    B. $1.67, \sqrt{5}, 0$

    C. $1.67, 0$

    D. 0

    E. None

49. **Which of the following is false?**

    A. Every rational number is a real number.

    B. Every imaginary number is a real number.

    C. Every integer is a whole number.

    D. Every integer is a real number.

    E. Every natural number is positive.

50. **Which selection below is NOT a real number?**

    A. -3

    B. $0.6666...$

    C. $\dfrac{\pi}{2}$

    D. $3 + \sqrt{2}$

    E. $3i$

51. **Simplify** $\sqrt{-9}$.

    A. -3

    B. $-3i$

    C. $3i$

    D. 3

    E. 0

52. **Simplify** $(i)(2i)(-3i)$.

    A. $6i$

    B. $-6i^3$

    C. $-6i$

    D. 0

    E. $6i^3$

53. Simplify i^{17}.

    A. $17i$

    B. i

    C. $-17i$

    D. $-i$

    E. 1

54. List the first four terms of the following sequence, beginning with $n=0$

    $$A_n = \frac{(-1)^n}{(n+1)!}$$

    A. $\frac{1}{2}, 1, \frac{3}{2}, 2$

    B. $-1, -\frac{1}{2}, 0, \frac{1}{2}$

    C. $0, 1, 2, 3$

    D. $1, -\frac{1}{2}, \frac{1}{6}, -\frac{1}{24}$

    E. $0, -1, -\frac{1}{2}, \frac{2}{3}$

55. Expand the following series and find the sum:

    $$\sum_{n=0}^{4} 2n$$

    A. 20

    B. 8

    C. 16

    D. 4

    E. 32

56. Write the series in sigma notation:
    -3 + 0 + 9 + 24 + 45 + 72 + 105

    A. $\sum_{a=0}^{6} 3a^2$

    B. $\sum_{a=0}^{6} 3a^2 - 3$

    C. $\sum_{a=0}^{6} a^2 - 3$

    D. $\sum_{a=1}^{6} 3a^2 - 1$

    E. $\sum_{a=0}^{5} a^2 - 3$

57. Find $\dfrac{8!}{6!2!}$

A. $\dfrac{2}{3}$

B. $\dfrac{4}{6}$

C. 28

D. 48

E. 24

58. Expand the binomial
$(2x+3y)^4$

A. $16x4+24x3y+36x2y2+54$
$xy3+81y42x4+6x3y+6x2$
$y2+6xy3+3y42x^4+6x^3y+$
$6x^2y^2+6xy^3+3y^4$

$2x^4+6x^3y+6x^2y^2+6xy^3+3y^4$

B. $16x^4+81y^4$

C. $16x^4+96x^3y+216x^2y^2$
$+216xy^3$
$+81y^4$

D. $16x^4+24x^3y^3+36x^2y^2+54x$
$y+81y^4$

E. $X^4+4x^3y+6x^2y^2+4xy^3+y^4$

59. Evaluate the determinant
of the matrix:
$$\begin{pmatrix} -2 & 4 \\ -4 & 3 \end{pmatrix}$$

A. 10

B. -24

C. 4

D. -10

E. 24

60. Evaluate the determinant
of the matrix for $y = 4$.
$$\begin{pmatrix} -5y & 3y \\ y-1 & y-3 \end{pmatrix}$$

A. 35

B. 12

C. -56

D. -12

E. 56

ANSWER KEY

Question Number	Correct Answer	Your Answer		Question Number	Correct Answer	Your Answer
1	A			31	D	
2	C			32	A	
3	C			33	B	
4	C			34	C	
5	D			35	E	
6	B			36	E	
7	A			37	B	
8	D			38	A	
9	C			39	C	
10	D			40	B	
11	C			41	C	
12	B			42	E	
13	D			43	D	
14	A			44	C	
15	A			45	B	
16	B			46	D	
17	D			47	E	
18	C			48	A	
19	A			49	E	
20	E			50	E	
21	B			51	C	
22	C			52	A	
23	B			53	B	
24	D			54	D	
25	E			55	A	
26	A			56	B	
27	D			57	C	
28	A			58	C	
29	B			59	A	
30	A			60	C	

RATIONALES

1.   Which of the following is a factor of the expression $9x^2 + 6x - 35$?

    A. $3x - 5$

    B. $3x - 7$

    C. $x + 3$

    D. $x - 2$

    E. $x - 3$

The answer is: A

The trinomial can be factored into two binomials, one with addition and one containing subtraction. The factors of 9 to use are 3 and 3 and 7 and 5 are used for 35. $(3x - 5)(3x + 7)$ checks when multiplying back through:

$9x^2 + 21x - 15x - 35 = 9x^2 + 6x - 35$

2.   Given $f(x) = 3x - 2$ and $g(x) = x^2$, determine $g(f(x))$.

    A. $3x^2 - 2$

    B. $9x^2 + 4$

    C. $9x^2 - 12x + 4$

    D. $3x^3 - 2$

    E. $9x^2 - 36$

The answer is: C

Evaluate: $g(f(x)) = g(3x - 2) = (3x - 2)^2$

Simplify by expanding: $(3x - 2)(3x - 2)$

$9x^2 - 6x - 6x + 4$ Which simplifies to choice C

3.   **Solve for *x*:** $18 = 4 + |2x|$

   A. $\{-11, 7\}$

   B. $\{-7, 0, 7\}$

   C. $\{-7, 7\}$

   D. $\{-11, 11\}$

   E. $\{-8, 8\}$

The answer is: C

First isolate the absolute value: $18 = 4 + |2x|$
$$14 = |2x|$$
Then use the definition of absolute value to set up and solve two equations:
$$2x = 14 \; or \; 2x = -14$$
$$x = 7, x = -7$$

4.   **Solve for *x* by factoring:** $2x^2 - 3x - 2 = 0$

   A. $x = (-1, 2)$

   B. $x = (0.5, -2)$

   C. $x = (-0.5, 2)$

   D. $x = (1, -2)$

   E. $x = (-2, 2)$

The answer is: C

Factor the trinomial into one binomial sum and one binomial difference:
$$(2x + 1)(x - 2)$$
Then set each factor equal to zero and solve for x:
$$2x + 1 = 0 \; or \; x - 2 = 0$$
$$x = -\frac{1}{2}, 2$$

5.   **Which of the following illustrates an inverse property?**

    A. $a+b=a-b$

    B. $a+b=b+a$

    C. $a+0=a$

    D. $a+(-a)=0$

    E. $b-a=0$

The answer is: D
Choice D represents the sum of a number and its opposite, or additive inverse. This illustrates the inverse property.

6.   **The conjugate of $4+5i$ is**

    A. $-4+5i$

    B. $4-5i$

    C. $4i+5$

    D. $4i-5$

    E. $-4-5i$

The answer is: B
For any complex number $a + bi$, the conjugate is defined as $a - bi$.

7.   **Simplify:** $(6+3i)-(4-2i)$

   A. $2+5i$

   B. $2+i$

   C. $10+5i$

   D. $2-2i$

   E. $10-5i$

The answer is: A
To add complex numbers, add the real parts together and the imaginary parts together. $(6 + 3i) + -(4 - 2i) = 6 + (-4) + 3i + 2i = 2 + 5i$

8.   **Simplify:** $\dfrac{10}{1+3i}$

   A. $-1.25(1-3i)$

   B. $1.25(1+3i)$

   C. $1+3i$

   D. $1-3i$

   E. $10+3i$

The answer is: D
A rational expression with an imaginary denominator must be simplified using the conjugate of the complex denominator:
$$\frac{10}{1+3i} \cdot \frac{1-3i}{1-3i} = \frac{10-30i}{1-9i^2} = \frac{10-30i}{1+9} = \frac{10-30i}{10} = 1-3i$$

9. **Solve** $(2b^3 \cdot b^2)^3$

    A. $3b^9$

    B. $2b^8$

    C. $8b^{15}$

    D. $2b^{18}$

    E. $8b^{18}$

The answer is: C

First simplify inside the parenthesis by adding exponents:
$$(2b^3 \cdot b^2)^3 = (2b^5)^3$$
Then raise to the third power, multiplying exponents:
$$(2b^5)^3 = 2^3 b^{15} = 8b^{15}$$

10. **Which of the following is incorrect?**

    A. $\left(x^2 y^3\right)^2 = x^4 y^6$

    B. $m^2(2n)^3 = 8m^2 n^3$

    C. $\dfrac{m^3 n^4}{m^2 n^2} = mn^2$

    D. $\left(x + y^2\right)^2 = x^2 + y^4$

    E. $\left(2s^{-4} w^4\right)\left(7sw^{-5}\right) = \dfrac{14}{s^3 w}$

The answer is: D

A power can distribute to a monomial, as seen in choices A and E, but not to a binomial. To find the correct answer expand and multiply:
$$\left(x + y^2\right)^2 = (x + y^2)(x + y^2) = x^2 + xy^2 + xy^2 + y^4$$

78

11. **Evaluate**

$$3^{\frac{1}{2}}\left(9^{\frac{1}{3}}\right)$$

   A. $27^{\frac{5}{6}}$

   B. $9^{\frac{7}{12}}$

   C. $3^{\frac{5}{6}}$

   D. $3^{\frac{6}{7}}$

   E. $9^{\frac{12}{7}}$

The answer is: C

Rewrite the expression with like bases. $3^{\frac{1}{2}}\left(9^{\frac{1}{3}}\right)=3^{\frac{1}{2}}\left(3^2\right)^{\frac{1}{3}}$

Then use exponent rules to combine the like bases. $3^{\frac{1}{2}}\left(3^2\right)^{\frac{1}{3}}=3^{\frac{1}{2}}\left(3^{\frac{2}{3}}\right)=3^{\left(\frac{3}{6}+\frac{4}{6}\right)}=3^{\frac{5}{6}}$

12.   **Simplify:**

$$\frac{4x^0 y^{-2} z^3}{4x}$$

A. $\dfrac{z^3}{y^2}$

B. $\dfrac{z^3}{y^2 x}$

C. $\dfrac{z^2}{y^3}$

D. $\dfrac{z^3}{x^2 y}$

E. $z^3 y^2$

The answer is: B

Initially, 4/4 reduces to 1 and x^0 also equals 1. Then the expression $\dfrac{y^{-2} z^3}{x} = \dfrac{z^3}{xy^2}$

13.   **The exponential equation** $2^5 = 32$ **can be written as:**

A. $\log_2(5) = 32$

B. $\log_{10}(32) = 5$

C. $\log_5(32) = 2$

D. $\log_2(32) = 5$

E. $\log_5(2) = 32$

The answer is: D

Logarithmic and exponential equations share the following relationship:
If $(base)^{exponent} = n$, then $\log_{(base)} n = exponent$.

14.   Which equation corresponds to the logarithmic statement $\log_x k = m$?

   A. $x^m = k$

   B. $k^m = x$

   C. $x^k = m$

   D. $m^x = k$

   E. $k^x = m$

The answer is: A

See explanation for question 13.

15. **Solve for** x:
$$\log_6(x-5)+\log_6 x = 2$$

A. $x = 9$

B. $x = 2, x = 7$

C. $x = 6$

D. $x = -2, x = -7$

E. $x = -4, x = -9$

The answer is: A

Use the log rule: $\log_b(a) + \log_b(c) = \log_b(ac)$ to simplify the equation.
$$\log_6(x-5)+\log_6 x = \log_6 x(x-5) = 2$$

Then rewrite the log as an exponential relationship and solve for x.

$$\log_6 x(x-5) = 2$$
$$6^2 = x(x-5)$$
$$36 = x^2 - 5x$$
$$0 = x^2 - 5x - 36$$
$$0 = (x-9)(x+4),\ x = 9\ or\ x = -4$$

However, this solution can yield extraneous solutions, so the answer must be checked.

$$\log_6(9-5)+\log_6 9\ ?\ 2$$
$$\log_6(4)(9)\ ?\ 2 \qquad\qquad \log_6(-4-5)+\log_6(-4)\ ?\ 2$$
$$\log_6 36 = 2$$

The second portion of the check fails, as the log of a negative number is undefined. So the only solution to the problem is x = 9

16. Solve for the slope m **and** y **-intercept:** $3x + 2y = 14$

A. $m = \dfrac{2}{3}, y = 5$

B. $m = -\dfrac{3}{2}, y = 7$

C. $m = \dfrac{3}{2}, y = -7$

D. $m = -\dfrac{2}{3}, y = -5$

E. $m = 2, y = 7$

The answer is: B

Put the given equation into slope intercept form, y=mx + b, where m is the slope and b the y intercept.

$$3x + 2y = 14$$
$$2y = -3x + 14$$
$$y = -\frac{3}{2}x + 7$$

17. Simplify: $-4(-4x - 1) - 4(7x + 3)$

A. $-44x + 16$

B. $12x - 16$

C. $44x - 16$

D. $-12x - 8$

E. $-11x + 2$

The answer is: D

Use the distributive property to begin simplifying; then collect like terms.

$$-4(-4x - 1) - 4(7x + 3)$$
$$16x + 4 - 28x - 12$$
$$-12x - 8$$

18.   Solve $-2x < 5$.

A. $x < -\dfrac{5}{2}$

B. $x > -\dfrac{2}{5}$

C. $x > -\dfrac{5}{2}$

D. $x > \dfrac{5}{2}$

E. $x < \dfrac{5}{2}$

The answer is: C

To solve the inequality, divide both sides by -2. This step, however, requires a reversal of the inequality symbol, resulting in choice C.

19. **Solve** $10 \le 3x + 4 \le 19$.

    A. $2 \le x \le 5$

    B. $-2 \le x \le 5$

    C. $x \le 5$

    D. $x \ge 2$

    E. $-5 \le x \le -2$

The answer is: A

The first equation solving step used to isolate the x is the subtraction of 4. In a conjunction, the subtraction, as well as the division of 3 following, must be performed on all three parts of the inequality.

$$10 \le 3x + 4 \le 19$$
$$6 \le 3x \le 15$$
$$2 \le x \le 5$$

20. **Solve for x:** $x^2 + 10x - 24 = 0$

    A.   (-5, 12)

    B.   (-10, 8)

    C.   (12, 2)

    D.   (10, 8)

    E.   (-12, 2)

The answer is: E

Factor the trinomial and set each factor equal to zero to solve for x.

$$x^2 + 10x - 24 = 0$$
$$(x + 12)(x - 2) = 0$$
$$x + 12 = 0 \; or \; x - 2 = 0$$

21.   **Find a quadratic equation with roots of 4 and -9.**

    A. $x^2 - 5x + 36 = 0$

    B. $x^2 + 5x - 36 = 0$

    C. $4x^2 - 9x - 5 = 0$

    D. $x^2 + 4x - 9 = 0$

    E. $5x^2 - 9x + 4 = 0$

The answer is: B

If r is a root of a polynomial, then (x – r) is a factor.

$$(x - 4)(x + 9) = 0$$

$$x^2 - 4x + 9x - 36 = 0$$

$$x^2 + 5x - 36 = 0$$

22. **Solve:** $4800 \leq 200x - 2x^2$

   A. $-40 \leq x \leq 40$

   B. $x \leq 40$

   C. $40 \leq x \leq 60$

   D. $x = 40$

   E. $x = -40$

The answer is: C

Start the solution process by setting the inequality less than zero.
$$2x^2 - 200x + 4800 \leq 0$$
One approach is to then graph the parabolic function on a calculator, and, after adjusting the window appropriately, find that the parabola is below the x axis , or less than zero, between 40 and 60. Alternatively, factor and solve the inequality: $2x^2 - 200x + 4800 \leq 0$
$$x^2 - 100x + 2400 \leq 0$$
$$(x - 40)(x - 60) \leq 0$$

But this work indicates that 40 and 60 are boundaries to a solution interval. Values must be tested in order to determine the actual values where the inequality is less than zero.

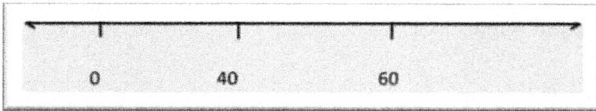

For instance, test a value greater than 60, like 70:

$2(70)^2 - 200(70) + 4800 = 600$ Which is greater than zero. So the solution does not exist in this interval. Continue with the remaining intervals as shown on the number line to conclude that the polynomial is less than zero between 40 and 60.

23.   **Solve:** $|3x + 2| = 4x + 5$

  A. $x = -3$

  B. $x = -1$

  C. $x = 3$

  D. $x = 1$

  E. $x = 6$

The answer is: B

Use the definition of absolute value to set up two equations.

$$3x + 2 = 4x + 5 \ or \ 3x + 2 = -4x - 5$$

$$-x = 3 \ or - 7x = 7$$

$$x = -3 \ or \ x = -1$$

Check for extraneous solutions:

$$|3x + 2| = 4x + 5 \qquad\qquad |3x + 2| = 4x + 5$$
$$|3(-3) + 2| \,?\, 4(-3) + 5 \qquad |3(-1) + 2| \,?\, 4(-1) + 5$$
$$|-9 + 2| \,?\, -12 + 5 \qquad\qquad |-3 + 2| \,?\, -4 + 5$$
$$7 \ne -7 \qquad\qquad\qquad\qquad 1 = 1$$

Therefore -3 is not a solution while -1 is.

24. Solve:

$$|3x-5|=\frac{1}{2}$$

A. $x=-\frac{11}{6},-\frac{3}{2}$

B. $x=-\frac{11}{6},\frac{3}{2}$

C. $x=\frac{11}{6},-\frac{3}{2}$

D. $x=\frac{11}{6},\frac{3}{2}$

E. $x=11,\frac{3}{2}$

The answer is: D

Use the definition of absolute value to set up two equations.

$$3x-5=\frac{1}{2} \qquad\qquad 3x-5=-\frac{1}{2}$$
$$3x=\frac{11}{2} \qquad\qquad 3x=\frac{9}{2}$$
$$x=\frac{11}{6} \qquad\qquad x=\frac{3}{2}$$

25. **Solve:**

$2|3x+9| < 36$

A. $x < -9$

B. $x > 3$

C. $3 < x < 9$

D. $-9 < x < -3$

E. $-9 < x < 3$

The answer is: E

First isolate the absolute value, then set up a conjunction to solve.

$$2|3x+9| < 36$$
$$|3x+9| < 18$$
$$-18 < 3x+9 < 18$$
$$-27 < 3x < 9$$
$$-9 < x < 3$$

26. **Solve for** x **and** y :

$4x+3y=-1$

$5x+4y=1$

A. $x=-7, y=9$

B. $x=7, y=-9$

C. $x=7, y=9$

D. $x=-7, y=-9$

E. $x=y=7$

The answer is: A

Using the elimination method: $4x+3y=-1 \xrightarrow{-4} -16x-12y=4$

$5x+4y=1 \xrightarrow{3} 15x+12y=3$

After combining the two new equations, -x = 7 or x = -7. Substitute into one equation to find y.

4(-7) + 3y = -1, y = 9. Therefore the solution to the system is (-7, 9).

27.   Which point is in the solution set for the system of inequalities below?

$$x - 7 < 1$$
$$y < 2x - 1$$

A. $(-1, -1)$

B. $(-2, -1)$

C. $(0, 1)$

D. $(0, -2)$

E. $(1, 1)$

The answer is: D

Only point D satisfies both equations algebraically: $0 - 7 < 1$, $-2 < 2(0) - 1$.
Additionally, a graph shows that only point D is within the shaded solution region. (Note that point E is on the line, which is not part of the solution region)

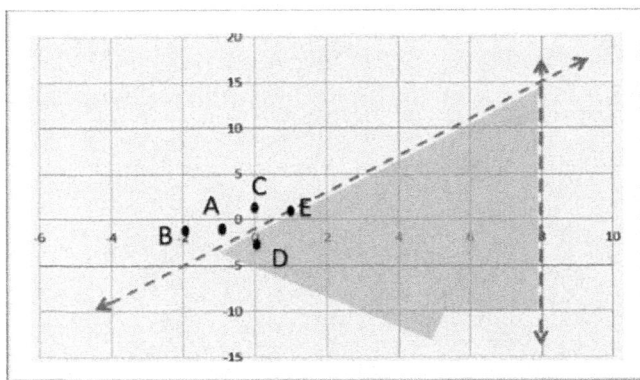

28.   **Solve:**

$3^{2x-1} = 27$

A. $x = 2$

B. $x = -3$

C. $x = -2$

D. $x = 3$

E. $x = \dfrac{2}{3}$

The answer is: A

Since $27 = 3^3$, the equation can be rewritten: $3^{2x-1} = 3^3$. With the same base on each side, the exponents must be equal. $2x - 1 = 3$, so $x = 2$.

29.   **Solve:**

$\log_b(x^2) = \log_b(2x - 1)$

A. $x = -2$

B. $x = 1$

C. $x = -1$

D. $x = 2$

E. $x = 4$

The answer is: B

Since the log is of the same base on each side of the equation, the arguments are equal.

$$x^2 = 2x - 1$$

$$x^2 - 2x + 1 = 0$$

$$(x - 1)(x - 1) = 0, x = 1$$

30. **Solve:**
$\log_2(x) + \log_2(x-2) = 3$

A. $x = 4$

B. $x = -4, 2$

C. $x = -4, -2$

D. $x = 4, -2$

E. $x = 2$

The answer is: A

Combine the log expressions into one using the product/sum rule:
$$\log_b(a) + \log_b(c) = \log_b(ac)$$
$$\log_2 x(x-2) = 3$$

Then rewrite the relationship exponentially.

$$2^3 = x(x-2)$$

$$8 = x^2 - 2x$$

$$0 = x^2 - 2x - 8$$

$$0 = (x-4)(x+2), x = 4, -2$$

However, when preparing to check the solutions, x cannot be a negative number as the log function is not defined over negative numbers. Check the positive value for x.

$$\log_2(4) + \log_2(4-2)\,?\,3$$
$$\log_2(4) + \log_2(2)\,?\,3$$
$$2 + 1 = 3$$

31. If $f(x) = -3x + 8$, find $f(5)$.

    A. 23

    B. -23

    C. 7

    D. -7

    E. 21

The answer is: D

Evaluate the function for x = 5. $f(5) = -3(5) + 8 = -15 + 8 = -7$

32. Find the zeros of the function $h(x) = \dfrac{x-9}{x+2}$.

    A. { 9 }

    B. { -2 }

    C. $\left\{ -\dfrac{9}{2} \right\}$

    D. { -2, 9 }

    E. This function has no zeros.

The answer is: A

The zero of a function is defined as the (x) input required to give the function a (y) value of zero. This function will be zero when the numerator has a value of zero: $x - 9 = 0, x = 9$. When the denominator of this function equals zero, at x = -2, the function will be undefined.

33.   **Which number line shows the solution to** $7x - 5 \geq 9x - 17$?

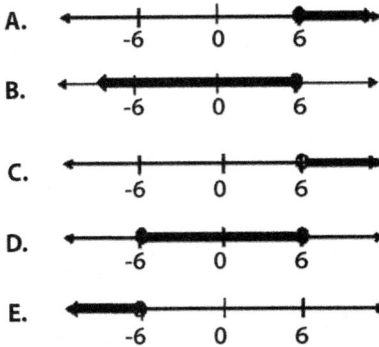

A.

B.

C.

D.

E.

The answer is: B

First gather all the x terms on one side of the inequality and the numbers on the other.

$$7x - 5 \geq 9x - 17$$

$$-2x \geq -12$$

When dividing both sides of an inequality by a negative number, the inequality sign is reversed. So division by -2 on both sides results in $x \leq 6$ which is graphed in choice B.

34.   Which graph represents the equation of $y = x^2 + 3x$?

A.

B.

C.

D.

E.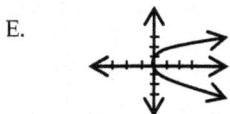

The answer is: C

Find the x intercepts of the graph by making y = 0 and solving for x.

$$0 = x^2 + 3x$$

$$0 = x(x + 3), x = 0 \ or \ x = -3$$

Therefore the x intercepts are (0, 0) and (0, -3) which are seen in the graph pictured in choice C.

35. Based on the given table, if $y_1 = x^3$, what is the equation for y_2?

x	-2	-1	0	1	2	3
y_1	-8	-1	0	1	8	27
y_2	-18	-11	-10	-9	-2	-17

A. $y_2 = x^5$

B. $y_2 = -x^3$

C. $y_2 = (-x)^3$

D. $y_2 = (x-10)^3$

E. $y_2 = x^3 - 10$

The answer is: E

When comparing each y_2 to each y_1, a difference of 10 is observed, resulting in choice E.

36. Identify the domain and range of the relation:

$$\{(2,-5),(4,31),(11,-11),(-21,3)\}$$

A. Domain is { -21 } range is { -11 }

B. Domain is { -5, 31, -11, 3 } range is { 2, 4, 11, 21 }.

C. Domain is { 11 } and range is { 31 }

D. Domain and range are indeterminate.

E. Domain is { 2, 4, 11, -21}, range is { -5, 31, -11, 3 }.

The answer is: E

In a set of ordered pairs, the domain is made up of the values for x, while the range consists of the y values.

37. **Determine the domain of**
   $y = -\sqrt{-2x+3}.$

   A. $x = 3$

   B. $x \leq \dfrac{3}{2}$

   C. $x > \dfrac{3}{2}$

   D. $x = 2$

   E. $x = 0$

The answer is: B

In order to keep the function defined over the real numbers, the radicand must remain non-negative.

$$-2x + 3 \geq 0$$

$$-2x \geq -3$$

$x \leq \frac{3}{2}$ as the inequality is reversed when dividing by a negative number.

38.   **For the function** $h(x)$ **whose graph is shown below, select the domain and range.**

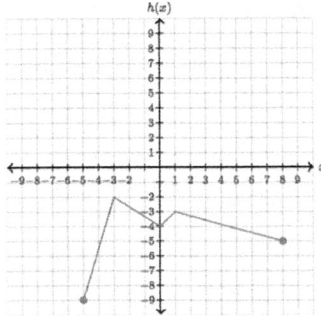

A.   Domain is $-5 \le x \le 8$, range is $-9 \le h \le -2$.

B.   Domain is -5, range is -5.

C.   Range is $-5 \le x \le 8$, domain is $-9 \le h \le 2$.

D.   Domain is $x \ge -5$, range is $h \ge -9$.

E.   Domain is 8, range is -2.

The answer is: A

Choice A represents the graphed x values for the domain, and the graphed y values for the range.

39.   **Given** $f(x) = 3x^2 - 7x + 5,$ **find** $f(-4)$.

A.   -71

B.   25

C.   81

D.   -25

E.   71

The answer is: C

Evaluate the function for x = -4

$f(-4) = 3(-4)^2 - 7(-4) + 5 = 3(16) + 28 + 5 = 81$

40. For $h(x) = 3x^2 + ax - 1,\ h(3) = 8,$ **find the value of** a.

    A. 6

    B. -6

    C. -18

    D. 18

    E. 27

The answer is: B

Evaluate the function for x = 3, then solve for a.

$$h(3) = 8 = 3(3)^2 + a(3) - 1$$
$$8 = 27 + 3a - 1$$
$$-18 = 3a$$
$$a = -6$$

41. **Given** $f(x) = 3x^2 - 7x + 5,$ **find** $\dfrac{f(x+h) - f(x)}{h}$

    A. $7h$

    B. $6xh - 7$

    C. $6x + 3h - 7$

    D. $3x + 6h + 7$

    E. $5x$

The answer is: C

$$\frac{f(x+h) - f(x)}{h} = \frac{3(x+h)^2 - 7(x+h) + 5 - [3x^2 - 7x + 5]}{h}$$
$$= \frac{3x^2 + 6xh + 3h^2 - 7x - 7h + 5 - 3x^2 + 7x - 5}{h}$$
$$= \frac{6xh + 3h^2 - 7h}{h}$$
$$= 6x + 3h - 7$$

42.   Find the x- and y- intercepts for $5x - 3y = 15$.

   A. $x = 0, y = 0$

   B. $x = -3, y = 5$

   C. $x = -1, y = 5$

   D. $x = -5, y = 3$

   E. $x = 3, y = -5$

The answer is: E

To find the x intercept, make y = 0: 5x – 3(0) =15, x = 3.

To find the y intercept, make x = 0: 5(0) – 3y = 15, y = -5

43.   **Which of the figures is a reflection of the triangle shown?**

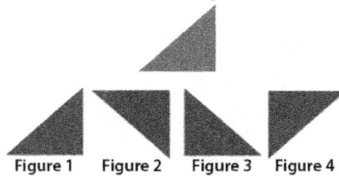

Figure 1   Figure 2   Figure 3   Figure 4

   A.   Figure 1 and Figure 4

   B.   Figure 4 and Figure 3

   C.   Figure 2 and Figure 1

   D.   Figures 2, 3 and 4

   E.   Figure 1 and Figure 2

The answer is: D

Figure 2 represents a vertical flip, or a reflection over the x axis. Figure 3 represents a horizontal flip, or a reflection over the y axis. Figure 4 is a result of both of these reflections applied.

44.   Name the transformation shown.

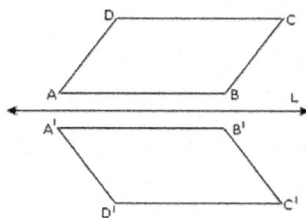

A.   Translation

B.   Rotation

C.   Reflection

D.   Dilation

E.   Cannot be determined

The answer is: C

The new image is created from a reflection over the x axis.

45.   Find the inverse of

$$y = 3x - 2.$$

A.

$$y = \frac{1}{3x - 2}$$

B.

$$y = \frac{x + 2}{3}$$

C.

$$x = \frac{y + 2}{3}$$

D. $y - 3x - 2 = 0$

E.

$$3x - y - 2 = 0$$

The answer is: B

To find the inverse of a function, switch the x and y, then solve for the "new" y.

$$x = 3y - 2$$
$$x + 2 = 3y$$
$$y = \frac{x+2}{3}$$

46.   Find the inverse of
$$f(x) = -\frac{1}{3}x + 1$$

A. $f^{-1}(x) = 1$

B. $f^{-1}(x) = 3x$

C. $f^{-1}(x) = 3x - 3$

D. $f^{-1}(x) = -3x + 3$

E. $f^{-1}(x) = x^2$

The answer is: D

Again, reverse the x and y, where f(x) = y.

$$y = -\frac{1}{3}x + 1$$
$$x = -\frac{1}{3}y + 1$$
$$x - 1 = -\frac{1}{3}y$$
$$-3x + 3 = y$$

Now the "new" y can be noted as $f^{-1}(x)$, which suggests the inverse of $f(x)$.

47. If $f(x) = 3x - 2$ and $g(x) = \dfrac{x}{3} + \dfrac{2}{3}$, which of the following is true:

 A. $f(x)$ is the inverse of $g(x)$.

 B. $f(x) = g^{-1}(x)$

 C. There is no connection between $f(x)$ and $g(x)$.

 D. $g(x) = f(x)$

 E. A and B

The answer is: E
Choice A and B each communicate that the two functions are inverses of each other. To prove this, derive one from the other, or show that $f(g(x)) = x = g(f(x))$

$$f(g(x)) = 3\left(\frac{x}{3} + \frac{2}{3}\right) - 2 = x + 2 - 2 = x$$
$$g(f(x)) = \frac{3x - 2}{3} + \frac{2}{3} = \frac{3x}{3} = x$$

48. **Identify the real numbers in the list:** $1.67, \pi, \sqrt{5}, 0$

 A. All

 B. $1.67, \sqrt{5}, 0$

 C. $1.67, 0$

 D. 0

 E. None

The answer is: A
All of the given numbers are real. (None are imaginary)

49.   **Which of the following is false?**

    A.   Every rational number is a real number.

    B.   Every imaginary number is a real number.

    C.   Every integer is a whole number.

    D.   Every integer is a real number.

    E.   Both B and C are false

The answer is: E
Choice B is false because no imaginary numbers are real. Choice C is false because some integers are negative, while whole numbers are zero or positive.

50.   **Which selection below is NOT a real number?**

    A.   -3

    B.   0.6666 …

    C. $\dfrac{\pi}{2}$

    D. $3+\sqrt{2}$

    E.   3i

The answer is: E
Choice E shows an imaginary number which is not real.

51. Simplify $\sqrt{-9}$.

    A.   -3

    B. $-3i$

    C. $3i$

    D.   3

    E.   0

The answer is: C

$$\sqrt{-9} = \sqrt{9} \cdot \sqrt{-1} = 3i$$

52. Simplify $(i)(2i)(-3i)$.

    A. $6i$

    B. $-6i^3$

    C. $-6i$

    D.   0

    E. $6i^3$

The answer is: A

$(i)(2i)(-3i) = -6i^3 = -6(-i) = 6i$

53.   Simplify i^{17}.

   A. $17i$

   B. i

   C. $-17i$

   D. $-i$

   E.   1

The answer is: B

$i^{17} = (i^4)^4 \cdot i = 1i = i$

54.   List the first four terms of the following sequence, beginning with $n = 0$.

$$A_n = \frac{(-1)^n}{(n+1)!}$$

   A. $\frac{1}{2}, 1, \frac{3}{2}, 2$

   B. $-1, -\frac{1}{2}, 0, \frac{1}{2}$

   C. $0, 1, 2, 3$

   D. $1, -\frac{1}{2}, \frac{1}{6}, -\frac{1}{24}$

   E. $0, -1, -\frac{1}{2}, \frac{2}{3}$

The answer is: D

Evaluate the sequence rule for n = 0, 1, 2, 3

$\frac{(-1)^0}{(0+1)!}, \frac{(-1)^1}{(1+1)!}, \frac{(-1)^2}{(2+1)!}, \frac{(-1)^3}{(3+1)!}$

$\frac{1}{(1)!}, \frac{-1}{(2)!}, \frac{1}{(3)!}, \frac{-1}{(4)!}$

$1, \frac{-1}{4}, \frac{1}{6}, \frac{-1}{24}$

55. Expand the following series and find the sum:

$$\sum_{n=0}^{4} 2n$$

A. 20

B. 8

C. 16

D. 4

E. 32

The answer is: A

The five terms in the expansion are $0 + 2 + 4 + 6 + 8$ so the sum is 20.

56. Write the series in sigma notation:
$$-3 + 0 + 9 + 24 + 45 + 72 + 105$$

A. $\sum_{a=0}^{6} 3a^2$

B. $\sum_{a=0}^{6} 3a^2 - 3$

C. $\sum_{a=0}^{6} a^2 - 3$

D. $\sum_{a=1}^{6} 3a^2 - 1$

E. $\sum_{a=0}^{5} a^2 - 3$

The answer is: B

Working backwards, substituting the start value into the rule for each sum, eliminates all but choice B. That is, choice B is the only rule where a_0 or a_1 matches the first listed term in the sum. Furthermore, evaluating the rule for $n = 0 - 6$ proves that all 7 terms match confirming that B is the correct choice.

57. Find $\dfrac{8!}{6!2!}$

    A. $\dfrac{2}{3}$

    B. $\dfrac{4}{6}$

    C. 28

    D. 48

    E. 24

The answer is: C

Most calculators can handle factorials of this size, however it is practical to know how to simplify an expression of this sort.

$$\frac{8!}{6!2!} = \frac{8 \cdot 7 \cdot 6!}{2 \cdot 6!} = \frac{8}{2} \cdot 7 = 4 \cdot 7 = 28$$

58.   Expand the binomial $(2x+3y)^4$

A. $16x^4 + 24x^3y + 36x^2y^2 + 54xy^3 + 81y^4$
      $2x^4 + 6x^3y + 6x^2y^2 + 6xy^3 + 3y^4$

B. $16x^4 + 81y^4$

C. $16x^4 + 96x^3y + 216x^2y^2 + 216xy^3 + 81y^4$

D. $16x^4 + 24x^3y^3 + 36x^2y^2 + 54xy + 81y^4$

E. $x^4 + 4x^3y + 6x^2y^2 + 4xy^3 + y^4$

The answer is: C

This problem can be expanded by binomial and trinomial multiplication, using coefficients of Pascal's Triangle, or following the Binomial Expansion Formula.

$(2x+3y)^4 = (2x+3y)^2 \cdot (2x+3y)^2$
$= (4x^2 + 12xy + 9y^2)(4x^2 + 12xy + 9y^2)$
$= 16x^4 + 48x^3y + 36x^2y^2 + 48x^3y + 144x^2y^2 + 108xy^3 + 36x^2y^2 + 108xy^3 + 81y^4$
$= 16x^4 + 96x^3y + 216x^2y^2 + 216xy^3 + 81y^4$

Check the third term using the Binomial Expansion Formula:

$$(a + b)^n = \sum_{k=0}^{n} {}_nC_k a^{n-k} b^k$$

To find the third term, k = 2. (since the formula starts with k = 0)
$(2x + 3y)^4:$ ${}_4C_2(2x)^{4-2}(3y)^2 = 6 \cdot 4x^2 \cdot 9y^2 = 216x^2y^2$

59.   Evaluate the determinant of the matrix:
$$\begin{pmatrix} -2 & 4 \\ -4 & 3 \end{pmatrix}$$

A.   10

B.   -24

C.   4

D.   -10

E.   24

The answer is: A

Given the matrix $\begin{pmatrix} a & b \\ c & d \end{pmatrix}$, the determinant can be calculated by $ad - cb$.

$(-2)(3) - (-4)(4) = -6 - (-16) = -6 + 16 = 10$

60.   **Evaluate the determinant of the matrix for** $y = 4.$ $\begin{pmatrix} -5y & 3y \\ y-1 & y-3 \end{pmatrix}$

A.   35

B.   12

C.   -56

D.   -12

E.   56

The answer is: C

First evaluate the matrix for y = 4.

$$\begin{pmatrix} -5(4) & 3(4) \\ 4-1 & 4-3 \end{pmatrix} = \begin{pmatrix} -20 & 12 \\ 3 & 1 \end{pmatrix}$$

Then use the determinant formula described above: $-20(1) - 3(12) = -56$

Description of the Examination

The Biology examination covers material that is usually taught in a one-year college general biology course. The subject matter tested covers the broad field of the biological sciences, organized into three major areas: molecular and cellular biology, organismal biology, and population biology.

The examination gives approximately equal weight to these three areas. The examination contains approximately 115 questions to be answered in 90 minutes. Some of these are pretest questions that will not be scored. Any time candidates spend on tutorials and providing personal information is in addition to the actual testing time.

Knowledge and Skills Required

Questions on the Biology examination require candidates to demonstrate one or more of the following abilities.

- Knowledge of facts, principles, and processes of biology
- Understanding the means by which information is collected, how it is interpreted, how one hypothesizes from available information, how one draws

conclusions and makes further predictions
- Understanding that science is a human endeavor with social consequences

The subject matter of the Biology examination is drawn from the following topics. The percentages next to the main topics indicate the approximate percentage of exam questions on that topic.

33% **Molecular and Cellular Biology**

- Chemical composition of organisms
- Simple chemical reactions and bonds
- Properties of water
- Chemical structure of carbohydrates, lipids, proteins, nucleic acids
- Origin of life

Cells

- Structure and function of cell organelles
- Properties of cell membranes
- Comparison of prokaryotic and eukaryotic cells

Enzymes

- Enzyme-substrate complex
- Roles of coenzymes
- Inorganic cofactors
- Inhibition and regulation

Energy transformations

- Glycolysis, respiration, anaerobic pathways
- Photosynthesis

Cell division

- Structure of chromosomes
- Mitosis, meiosis, and cytokinesis in plants and animals

Chemical nature of the gene

- Watson-Crick model of nucleic acids
- DNA replication
- Mutations
- Control of protein synthesis: transcription, translation, posttranscriptional processing
- Structural and regulatory genes
- Transformation
- Viruses

34% **Organismal Biology**

- Structure and function in plants with emphasis on angiosperms
- Root, stem, leaf, flower, seed, fruit
- Water and mineral absorption and transport
- Food translocation and storage
- Plant reproduction and development
- Alternation of generations in ferns, conifers, and flowering plants

- Gamete formation and fertilization
- Growth and development: hormonal control
- Tropisms and photoperiodicity

Structure and function in animals with emphasis on vertebrates

- Major systems (e.g., digestive, gas exchange, skeletal, nervous, circulatory, excretory, immune)
- Homeostatic mechanisms
- Hormonal control in homeostasis and reproduction

Animal reproduction and development

- Gamete formation, fertilization
- Cleavage, gastrulation, germ layer formation, differentiation of organ systems
- Experimental analysis of vertebrate development
- Extraembryonic membranes of vertebrates
- Formation and function of the mammalian placenta

- Blood circulation in the human embryo

Principles of heredity

- Mendelian inheritance (dominance, segregation, independent assortment)
- Chromosomal basis of inheritance
- Linkage, including sex-linked
- Polygenic inheritance (height, skin color)

33%   **Population Biology**

Principles of ecology

- Energy flow and productivity in ecosystems
- Biogeochemical cycles
- Population growth and regulation (natality, mortality, competition, migration, density, r- and K-selection)
- Community structure, growth, regulation (major biomes and succession)
- Habitat (biotic and abiotic factors)
- Concept of niche
- Island biogeography
- Evolutionary ecology (life history

strategies, altruism, kin selection)

Principles of evolution

- History of evolutionary concepts
- Concepts of natural selection (differential reproduction, mutation, Hardy-Weinberg equilibrium, speciation, punctuated equilibrium)
- Adaptive radiation
- Major features of plant and animal evolution
- Concepts of homology and analogy
- Convergence, extinction, balanced polymorphism, genetic drift
- Classification of living organisms
- Evolutionary history of humans

Principles of behavior

- Stereotyped, learned social behavior
- Societies (insects, birds, primates)

Social biology

- Human population growth (age composition, birth and fertility rates, theory of demographic transition)
- Human intervention in the natural world (management of resources, environmental pollution)
- Biomedical progress (control of human reproduction, genetic engineering)

SAMPLE TEST

DIRECTIONS: Read each item and select the best response.

1. **Which is not true about a cell membrane?**

   A. It is made from phospholipids

   B. Both plant and animal cells have a cell membrane.

   C. The cell wall is the same as the cell membrane in plants.

   D. It controls the passage of nutrients within a cell.

   E. It contains embedded proteins that help with passage.

2. **Microorganisms use all but which of the following for locomotion?**

   A. Pseudopods

   B. Flagella

   C. Cilia

   D. Pili

   E. Villi

3. **Which of the following does not possess eukaryotic cells?**

   A. Bacteria

   B. Protists

   C. Fungi

   D. Animals

   E. Plants

4. **Which of the following groups of organisms is comprised of those with one cell and no nuclear membrane?**

   A. Monera

   B. Protista

   C. Fungi

   D. Algae

   E. Plantae

5. Which of these are found on the outside of the rough endoplasmic reticulum?

A. Vacuoles

B. Mitochondria

C. Microfilaments

D. Ribosomes

E. Flagella

6. Identify the correct sequence of organization of living things.

A. cell – organelle – organ – tissue – organ system – organism

B. cell – tissue – organ – organelle – organ system – organism

C. organelle – cell – tissue – organ – organ system – organism

D. organ system – tissue – organelle – cell – organism – organ

E. organism – organ system – tissue – cell – organelle – organ

7. Which of these is not a characteristic shared by all living things?

A. movement

B. made of cells

C. metabolism

D. reproduction

E. respond to stimuli

8. What is the purpose of the Golgi apparatus?

A. To break down proteins

B. To break down fats

C. To make carbohydrates.

D. To provide the cell with energy

E. To sort, modify and package molecules

9. **What do amyloplasts do?**
   (Molecular & Cell Biology)

   A. Store starch in a plant cell

   B. Remove waste in animal cells

   C. Produce green and yellow pigment

   D. Aid in photosynthesis.

   E. Provide energy for metabolism

10. **Which of the following does not belong to the domain Archaea?**

    A. Methanogens

    B. Extreme Halophiles

    C. Thermoacidophiles

    D. Bacteriophiles

    E. Sulfobales

11. **The first cells that evolved on earth were probably of which type?**

    A. autotrophic

    B. eukaryotic

    C. heterotrophic

    D. prokaryotic

    E. endosymbiotic

12. **During which part of photosynthesis is oxygen given off?**

    A. light reactions

    B. dark reactions

    C. Krebs cycle

    D. reduction of NAD+ to NADH

    E. phosphorylation

13. Bacteria commonly reproduce by a process called binary fission. Which of the following best defines this process?

   A. Viral vectors carry DNA to new bacteria.

   B. DNA from one bacterium enters another.

   C. DNA doubles and the bacterial cell divides.

   D. DNA from dead cells is absorbed into bacteria.

   E. Bacteria merge with others to form new species.

14. Which tool is best for studying the individual parts of cells?

   A. ultracentrifuge

   B. phase-contrast microscope

   C. CAT scan

   D. electron microscope

   E. light microscope

15. Which of these classifications includes the thermoacidophiles?

   A. Plantae

   B. Animalia

   C. Bacteria

   D. Protista

   E. Archaea

16. Which of the following is not part of the cytoskeleton?

   A. vacuoles

   B. microfilaments

   C. microtubules

   D. intermediate filaments

   E. motor proteins

17. Of what are viruses made?

    A. A protein coat surrounding a nucleic acid.

    B. RNA and protein surrounded by a cell wall.

    C. A nucleic acid surrounding a protein coat.

    D. Protein surrounded by DNA.

    E. A lipid bilayer surrounding a protein coat and RNA.

18. Which of these are used to classify protists into their major groups?

    A. Their method of obtaining nutrition.

    B. Their method of reproduction.

    C. Their use of metabolism.

    D. Their form and function.

    E. Their means of locomotion.

19. Replication of chromosomes occurs during which phase of the cell cycle?

    A. prophase

    B. interphase

    C. metaphase

    D. anaphase

    E. metaphase

20. Which of these events occurs during telophase in a plant cell?

    A. the chromosomes are doubled

    B. a cell plate forms

    C. crossing over occurs

    D. a cleavage furrow develops

    E. spindle fibers become visible

21. What is the stage of mitosis seen in the diagram?

    A. anaphase

    B. metaphase

    C. telophase

    D. prophase

    E. interphase

22. What is the stage of mitosis shown in the diagram?

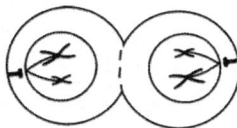

    A. prophase

    B. telophase

    C. anaphase

    D. metaphase

    E. interphase

23. What is the stage of mitosis shown in the diagram?

A. interphase

B. metaphase

C. prophase

D. telophase

E. anaphase

24. Which of the following is a monomer?

A. RNA

B. glycogen

C. DNA

D. amino acid

E. lipid

25. Which of the following does not affect enzyme rate?

A. increase of temperature

B. amount of substrate

C. pH

D. size of the cell

E. concentration of enzyme

26. All but which one of the following is true of a cell membrane?

A. It contains polar and nonpolar phospholipids.

B. It only uses active transport to move molecules across it.

C. It contains cholesterol.

D. It has proteins imbedded within it.

E. It is selectively permeable to many substances.

27. **Which of these describes facilitated diffusion?**

   A. It requires energy.

   B. It only happens in plant cells.

   C. It only allows molecules to leave a cell but not to enter it.

   D. It produces a significant amount of energy for the cell.

   E. It needs a transport molecule to pass through the membrane.

28. **What is not true of enzymes?**

   A. They are the most diverse of all proteins.

   B. They act on a substrate.

   C. They work at a wide range of pH.

   D. They are temperature-dependent.

   E. They have specialized functions.

29. **Which of these is necessary for diffusion to occur?**

   A. carrier proteins

   B. energy

   C. water molecules

   D. a cell membrane

   E. a concentration gradient

30. **Which is an example of the use of energy to move a substance through a membrane from areas of low concentration to areas of high concentration?**

   A. osmosis

   B. active transport

   C. exocytosis

   D. phagocytosis

   E. facilitated diffusion

31. A plant cell is placed in salt water. What is the resulting movement of water out of the cell called?

    A. facilitated diffusion

    B. diffusion

    C. transpiration

    D. osmosis

    E. active transport

32. **What are the monomers of polysaccharides?**

    A. Nucleotides

    B. Amino acids

    C. Polypeptides

    D. Fatty acids

    E. Simple sugars

33. **Which type of cell would contain the most mitochondria?**

    A. muscle cell

    B. nerve cell

    C. epithelial cell

    D. blood cell

    E. bone cell

34. According to the fluid-mosaic model of the cell membrane, of what are membranes composed?

    A. Phospholipid bilayers with proteins embedded in the layers.

    B. One layer of phospholipids with cholesterol embedded in the layer.

    C. Two layers of protein with lipids embedded in the layers.

    D. DNA and fluid proteins with carbohydrates embedded in the layer.

    E. Glycerol and RNA with carbohydrates embedded in the layer.

35. **Which is the correct statement regarding the human nervous system and the human endocrine system?**

A. The nervous system maintains homeostasis whereas the endocrine system does not.

B. Endocrine glands produce neurotransmitters whereas nerves produce hormones.

C. Nerve signals travel on neurons whereas hormones travel through the blood.

D. The nervous system involves chemical transmission whereas the endocrine system does not.

E. The nervous system produces physiological responses whereas the endocrine produces behavioral.

36. **Which process generates the most ATP?**

A. fermentation

B. glycolysis

C. the Calvin cycle

D. the Krebs cycle

E. chemiosmosis

37. **Which of these is a function of the cardiovascular system?**

A. Move oxygenated blood around the body

B. Oxygenate the blood through gas exchange

C. Act as an exocrine system

D. Flush toxins out of the body

E. Transport signals from the brain

38. Which of these is not a part of the nervous system?

    A. brain

    B. spinal cord

    C. axons

    D. venules

    E. cochlea

39. Organisms need to maintain a constant internal environment to survive. Which of these is a method by which they achieve this?

    A. respiration

    B. reproduction

    C. depolarization

    D. repolarization

    E. thermoregulation

40. Which of these controls the body's endocrine mechanisms?

    A. feedback loops

    B. control molecules

    C. neurochemicals

    D. neurotransmitters

    E. behavioral responses

41. What is the gland that regulates the calcium in the body?

    A. Thyroid gland

    B. Parathyroid gland

    C. Hypothalamus

    D. Pituitary gland

    E. Pancreas

42. Which of these steroids is not created in the gonads?

    A. Testosterone

    B. Estrogen

    C. Progesterone

    D. ACTH

    E. FSH

43. **What is the most common neurotransmitter?**

    A. epinephrine

    B. serotonin

    C. acetyl choline

    D. norepinephrine

    E. oxytocin

44. **Food is carried through the digestive tract by a series of wave-like contractions. What is this process is called?**

    A. peristalsis

    B. chyme

    C. digestion

    D. absorption

    E. depolarization

45. **Which of these must muscles pull on in order to initiate movement?**

    A. skin

    B. bones

    C. joints

    D. ligaments

    E. bursa

46. **Hormones are essential to the regulation of reproduction. What organ is responsible for the release of hormones for sexual maturity?**

    A. pituitary gland

    B. hypothalamus

    C. pancreas

    D. thyroid gland

    E. pineal gland

47. **What is the type of muscle in the human body that is voluntary?**

    A. Cardiac

    B. Sarcomere

    C. Smooth

    D. Skeletal

    E. Actin

48.   The wrist is an example of
      what kind of joint?

      A.   Ball and socket

      B.   Pivot

      C.   Stationary

      D.   Hinge

      E.   Gliding

49.   What is the waterproofing
      protein in the skin called?

      A.   actin

      B.   epidermis

      C.   collagen

      D.   sebum

      E.   keratin

50.   What is the muscular
      adaptation called that is
      used to move food
      through the digestive
      system?

      A.   peristalsis

      B.   passive transport

      C.   voluntary action

      D.   bulk transport

      E.   endocytosis

51.   What is the role of
      neurotransmitters in nerve
      action?

      A.   to turn off the sodium
           pump

      B.   to turn off the calcium
           pump

      C.   to send impulses to
           neurons

      D.   to send impulses
           around the body

      E.   to send impulses from
           axon to dendrite

52.   Fats are broken down by
      which substance?

      A.   bile produced in the
           gall bladder

      B.   lipase produced in the
           gall bladder

      C.   glucagons produced in
           the liver

      D.   amylase produces in
           the gall bladder

      E.   bile produced in the
           liver

53. **Where does fertilization in humans usually occurs?**

   A. uterus

   B. ovary

   C. fallopian tubes

   D. vagina

   E. epididymis

54. **Which of these is lacking in the dermis layer of skin?**

   A. sweat glands

   B. keratin

   C. hair follicles

   D. blood vessels

   E. living cells

55. **A school age boy had the chicken pox as a baby. Why will he most likely not get this disease again?**

   A. passive immunity

   B. vaccination

   C. antibiotics

   D. active immunity

   E. antigen production

56. **What is any foreign particle called that causes an immune reaction?**

   A. an antigen

   B. a histocompatibity complex

   C. an antibody

   D. a vaccine

   E. a bacteriophage

57. **Which of these statements describes the polymerase chain reaction?**

   A. It is a group of polymerases.

   B. It is a technique for amplifying DNA.

   C. It is a primer for DNA synthesis.

   D. It is a way to synthesize polymerase.

   E. It is a series of genetic mutations.

58. Which part of a DNA nucleotide can vary?

    A. deoxyribose

    B. phosphate group

    C. hydrogen bonds

    D. sugar

    E. nitrogenous base

59. A DNA strand has the base sequence of TCAGTA. Its DNA complement would have which of the following sequences?

    A. ATGACT

    B. TCAGTA

    C. AGUCAU

    D. AGTCAT

    E. TCTGTA

60. Which of these carries amino acids to the ribosome during protein synthesis?

    A. messenger RNA

    B. ribosomal RNA

    C. transfer RNA

    D. DNA

    E. RNA

61. A protein is sixty amino acids in length. This requires a coded DNA sequence of how many nucleotides?

    A. 20

    B. 30

    C. 120

    D. 180

    E. 240

62. A DNA molecule has the sequence of ACTATG. What is the anticodon of this molecule?

    A. UGAUAC

    B. ACUAUG

    C. TGATAC

    D. ACTATG

    E. CTGCGA

63. What is the general term for a change that affects the sequence of bases in a gene?

    A. deletion

    B. polyploid

    C. mutation

    D. duplication

    E. substitution

64. Segments of DNA can be transferred from the DNA of one organism to another through the use of which of the following?

    A. bacterial plasmids

    B. viruses

    C. chromosomes from frogs

    D. plant DNA

    E. Okazaki fragments

65. What is the enzyme that unwinds DNA during replication?

    A. DNAse

    B. DNA replicase

    C. DNA helicase

    D. DNA topoisomerases

    E. DNA polymerase

66. What is a small circular piece of DNA called that contains accessory DNA?

    A. mitochondrial DNA

    B. messenger RNA

    C. transfer DNA

    D. Okazaki fragment

    E. plasmid

67. In DNA, adenine bonds with _____, while cytosine bonds with _____.

    A. thymine/guanine

    B. adenine/cytosine

    C. cytosine/uracil

    D. guanine/thymine

    E. uracil/adenine

68. Which protein structure consists of the coils and folds of polypeptide chains?

    A. secondary structure

    B. quaternary structure

    C. tertiary structure

    D. primary structure

    E. quinary structure

69. What can be said about homozygous individuals?

    A. They have two different alleles.

    B. They are of the same species.

    C. They exhibit the same features.

    D. They have a pair of identical alleles.

    E. They produce identical offspring.

70. The term "phenotype" refers to which of the following?

A. a condition that is heterozygous

B. the genetic makeup of an individual

C. a condition that is homozygous

D. how the genotype is expressed

E. from which parent the traits were inherited

71. The ratio of brown-eyed to blue-eyed children from the mating of a blue-eyed male to a heterozygous brown-eyed female is expected to be which of the following?

A. 3:1

B. 2:2

C. 1:0

D. 1:2

E. 0:4

72. Which of these defines the Law of Segregation defined by Gregor Mendel?

A. After meiosis, each new cell will contain an allele that is recessive.

B. Only one of two alleles is expressed in a heterozygous organism.

C. The allele expressed is always the dominant allele.

D. Alleles of one trait do not affect the inheritance of alleles on another chromosome.

E. When sex cells form, the two alleles that determine a trait will end up on different gametes.

73. Which of the following is an example of the incomplete dominance that occurs when a white flower is crossed with a red flower?

A. pink flowers

B. red flowers

C. white flowers

D. red and white flowers

E. white and pink flowers

74. A child with type O blood has a father with type A blood and a mother with type B blood. The genotypes of the parents respectively would be which of the following?

A. AA and BO

B. AO and BO

C. AA and BB

D. AO and OO

E. OO and AB

75. Crossing over, which increases genetic diversity, occurs during which stage(s) of meiosis?

A. telophase II in meiosis

B. metaphase in mitosis

C. interphase in meiosis

D. prophase I in meiosis

E. metaphase II in meiosis

76. ABO blood grouping is an example of which type of allele dominance?

A. Autosomal dominance

B. Incomplete dominance

C. Somatic dominance

D. Complete dominance

E. Codominance

77. In a Punnett square with a single trait, what are the ratios of genotypes produced between two heterozygous individuals?

   A. 1:2:2

   B. 2:1:1

   C. 1:1:1

   D. 1:2:1

   E. 2:2:2

78. What is the term for an organism's genetic makeup?

   A. Heterozygote

   B. Genotype

   C. Phenotype

   D. Homozygote

   E. Dominance

79. Which of these represents a genetic engineering advancement in the medical field?

   A. stem cell reproduction

   B. pesticides

   C. degradation of harmful chemicals

   D. antibiotics

   E. gene therapy

80. Which of the following is not true regarding restriction enzymes?

   A. They aid in transcombination procedures.

   B. They are used in genetic engineering.

   C. They are named after the bacteria in which they naturally occur.

   D. They identify and splice certain base sequences on DNA.

   E. They can be produced by certain lipids during DNA replication.

81. Which of these processes is not one of the modern uses of DNA?

    A. PCR technology

    B. Gene therapy

    C. Cloning

    D. Genetic Alignment

    E. Transgenic organisms

82. Which statement best represents gel electrophoresis?

    A. It isolates fragments of DNA for scientific purposes.

    B. It cannot be used in proteins.

    C. It requires the polymerase chain reaction.

    D. It only separates DNA by size.

    E. It uses different charged particles to color the bands.

83. What is the term that describes the duplication of genetic material into another cell?

    A. replicating

    B. cell duplication

    C. transgenics

    D. genetic restructuring

    E. cloning

84. What does gel electrophoresis use to separate the DNA?

    A. the amount of current

    B. the size of the molecule

    C. the positive charge of the molecule

    D. the solubility of the gel

    E. the source of the DNA

85. **Which of these is a result of reproductive isolation?**

   A. extinction

   B. migration

   C. fossilization

   D. speciation

   E. radiation

86. **Which of these is true about natural selection?**

   A. It acts on an individual genotype.

   B. It is not currently happening.

   C. It is only an animal phenomenon.

   D. It acts on the individual phenotype.

   E. It is used to prevent overpopulation.

87. **How does diversity aid a population?**

   A. Individuals are better able to survive.

   B. Mates are attracted to a diverse population.

   C. Potential mates like conformity.

   D. It increases the DNA differences in the population.

   E. It provides possible improvements to the population.

88. **Which statement is not true about diversity?**

   A. Without diversity there would be extinction.

   B. Diversity is increasing all the time.

   C. Fossil evidence supports diversity.

   D. Sexual reproduction encourages more diversity.

   E. Skeletons are too similar to allow for diversity.

89. Which of these ideas was a major part of Darwin's evolutionary theory?

    A. Punctualism

    B. Gradualism

    C. Equilibrium

    D. Convergency

    E. Altruism

90. Which statement is not true about reproductive isolation?

    A. It prevents populations from exchanging genes.

    B. It can occur by preventing fertilization.

    C. It can result in speciation.

    D. It happens more often on the mainland.

    E. It produces offspring with unique phenotypes

91. Which idea is true about members of the same species?

    A. They look identical.

    B. They never change.

    C. They reproduce successfully within their group.

    D. They live in the same geographic location.

    E. They have very dissimilar genotypes.

92. Which of the following factors will affect the Hardy-Weinberg law of equilibrium, leading to evolutionary change?

   A. no mutations

   B. non-random mating

   C. no immigration or emigration

   C. large population

   E. small individual species

93. If a population is in Hardy-Weinberg equilibrium and the frequency of the recessive allele is 0.3, what percentage of the population is expected to be heterozygous?

   A. 9%

   B. 49%

   C. 42%

   D. 21%

   E. 7%

94. Which aspect of science does not support evolution?

   A. comparative anatomy

   B. organic chemistry

   C. comparison of DNA among organisms

   D. analogous structures

   E. embryology

95. In which of these does evolution occurs?

   A. individuals

   B. populations

   C. organ systems

   D. cells

   E. ecosystems

96. Which process contributes most to the large variety of living things in the world today?

    A. meiosis

    B. asexual reproduction

    C. mitosis

    D. alternation of generations

    E. reproductive isolation

97. Which of the following gases was a major part of the primitive Earth atmosphere?

    A. fluorine

    B. methane

    C. oxygen

    D. krypton

    E. argon

98. What is a major principle of the Endosymbiotic Theory?

    A. Birds and dinosaurs share a common ancestor.

    B. Animals evolved in close relationships with one another.

    C. Prokaryotes arose from eukaryotes.

    D. Inorganic compounds are the basis of living things.

    E. Eukaryotes arose from very simple prokaryotes.

99. The wing of a bird, the human arm, and the pectoral fluke of a whale all have the same bone structure. What are these structures called?

   A. polymorphic structures

   B. homologous structures

   C. vestigial structures

   D. analogous structures

   E. allopatric structures

100. Which of the following is not an abiotic factor?

   A. temperature

   B. rainfall

   C. soil quality

   D. predation

   E. wind speed

101. What is not true about cladistics?

   A. It is the study of phylogenetic relationships of organisms.

   B. It involves a branching diagram that uses the development of novel traits to separate groups of organisms.

   C. It distinguishes between the relative importance of the traits.

   D. It shows when traits developed with respect to other traits.

   E. It indicates which organisms are most closely related to each other and what their common ancestors were.

102. If DDT were present in an ecosystem, which of the following organisms would have the highest concentration in its body?

   A. herring

   B. diatom

   C. zooplankton

   D. salmon

   E. osprey

103. What eats secondary consumers?

   A. Producers

   B. Tertiary consumers

   C. Primary consumers

   D. Decomposers

   E. Detritivores

104. Which statement is true about the water cycle?

   A. Two percent of the water is fixed and unavailable.

   B. 75% of available water is groundwater.

   C. The water cycle is driven by the ocean currents.

   D. Surface water percolates up from underground springs.

   E. New water is being added into the cycle all the time.

105. **Which statement about the carbon cycle is false?**

   A. Ten percent of all available carbon is in the air.

   B. Carbon dioxide is fixed by glycosylation.

   C. Plants fix carbon in the form of glucose.

   D. Animals release carbon through respiration.

   E. Most atmospheric carbon comes from the decay of dead organisms.

106. **What is the impact of sulfur oxides and nitrogen oxides in the environment when they react with water?**

   A. ammonia

   B. acidic precipitation

   C. sulfuric acid

   D. global warming

   E. greenhouse effect

107. **Which term is not associated with the water cycle?**

   A. precipitation

   B. transpiration

   C. fixation

   D. evaporation

   E. runoff

108. **Which of the following is a density dependent factor that affects a population?**

   A. temperature

   B. rainfall

   C. predation

   D. soil nutrients

   E. wind speed

109. **High humidity and temperature stability are present in which of the following biomes?**

A. taiga

B. deciduous forest

C. desert

D. tropical rain forest

E. coniferous forest

110. **Which trophic level has the highest ecological efficiency?**

A. decomposers

B. producers

C. tertiary consumers

D. secondary consumers

E. primary consumers

111. **From where does the oxygen created in photosynthesis come?**

A. carbon dioxide

B. chlorophyll

C. glucose

D. carbon monoxide

E. water

112. **Which of the following is true of decomposers?**

A. Decomposers recycle the carbon accumulated in durable organic material.

B. They take nitrogen out of the soil to use for food.

C. Decomposers absorb nutrients from the air to maintain their metabolisms.

D. Decomposers belong to the Genus *Escherichia*.

E. They are able to use the Sun to produce their own energy.

113. A clownfish is protected by a sea anemone's tentacles, and in turn, the anemone receives uneaten food from the clownfish. What type of symbiosis is exemplified by this example?

   A. mutualism

   B. parasitism

   C. commensalism

   D. competition

   E. amensalism

114. Which of these is most likely to happen in order for primary succession to occur?

   A. nutrient enrichment

   B. a forest fire

   C. bare rock is exposed after a water table recedes

   D. a housing development is built

   E. a farmer stops cultivating her fields

115. What is the Mendelian law called that states that only one of the two possible alleles from each parent is passed on to the offspring?

   A. The Mendelian Law

   B. The Law of Independent Assortment

   C. The Law of Segregation

   D. The Allele Law

   E. The Law of Dominance and Recessiveness

BIOLOGY

ANSWER KEY

Question Number	Correct Answer	Your Answer	Question Number	Correct Answer	Your Answer	Question Number	Correct Answer	Your Answer
1.	C		41.	B		81.	D	
2.	E		42.	D		82.	A	
3.	A		43.	C		83.	E	
4.	A		44.	A		84.	B	
5.	D		45.	B		85.	D	
6.	C		46.	B		86.	D	
7.	A		47.	D		87.	E	
8.	E		48.	B		88.	E	
9.	A		49.	E		89.	B	
10.	D		50.	A		90.	D	
11.	D		51.	C		91.	C	
12.	A		52.	E		92.	B	
13.	C		53.	C		93.	C	
14.	D		54.	B		94.	B	
15.	E		55.	D		95.	B	
16.	A		56.	A		96.	A	
17.	A		57.	B		97.	B	
18.	D		58.	E		98.	E	
19.	B		59.	D		99.	B	
20.	B		60.	C		100.	D	
21.	B		61.	D		101.	C	
22.	B		62.	D		102.	E	
23.	E		63.	C		103.	B	
24.	D		64.	A		104.	A	
25.	D		65.	C		105.	B	
26.	B		66.	E		106.	B	
27.	E		67.	A		107.	C	
28.	C		68.	A		108.	C	
29.	E		69.	D		109.	D	
30.	B		70.	D		110.	B	
31.	D		71.	B		111.	E	
32.	E		72.	E		112.	A	
33.	A		73.	A		113.	A	
34.	A		74.	B		114.	C	
35.	C		75.	D		115.	B	
36.	E		76.	E				
37.	A		77.	D				
38.	D		78.	B				
39.	E		79.	E				
40.	A		80.	A				

RATIONALES

1.   **Which is not true about a cell membrane?**

   A.   It is made from phospholipids

   B.   Both plant and animal cells have a cell membrane.

   C.   The cell wall is the same as the cell membrane in plants.

   D.   It controls the passage of nutrients within a cell.

   E.   It contains embedded proteins that help with passage.

The answer is C.
Both plants and animals have cell membranes but plant cells also have an outer cell wall to give it structure.

2.   **Microorganisms use all but which of the following for locomotion?**

   A.   Pseudopods

   B.   Flagella

   C.   Cilia

   D.   Pili

   E.   Villi

The answer is E.
Pseudopods, pili, flagella and cilia are used by microorganisms for movement. Vili are used in the small intestine to increase surface area for absorption.

3.   Which of the following does not possess eukaryotic cells?

   A.   Bacteria

   B.   Protists

   C.   Fungi

   D.   Animals

   E.   Plants

The answer is A.
Eukaryotic cells are found in protists, fungi, plants and animals but not in bacteria.

4.   Which of the following groups of organisms is comprised of those with one cell and no nuclear membrane?

   A.   Monera

   B.   Protista

   C.   Fungi

   D.   Algae

   E. Plantae

The answer is A.
Monera is the only kingdom that is made up of unicellular organisms with no nucleus. Algae are protists because it is made up of one type of tissue and it has a nucleus.

5. **Which of these are found on the outside of the rough endoplasmic reticulum?**

    A. Vacuoles

    B. Mitochondria

    C. Microfilaments

    D. Ribosomes

    E. Flagella

The answer is D.
Rough endoplasmic reticulum is defined as such because of the occurrence of ribosomes on its surface.

6. **Identify the correct sequence of organization of living things.**

    A. cell – organelle – organ – tissue – organ system – organism

    B. cell – tissue – organ – organelle – organ system – organism

    C. organelle – cell – tissue – organ – organ system – organism

    D. organ system – tissue – organelle – cell – organism – organ

    E. organism – organ system – tissue – cell – organelle – organ

The answer is C.
An organism, such as a human, is comprised of several organ systems such as the circulatory and nervous systems. These organ systems consist of many organs including the heart and the brain. These organs are made of tissue such as cardiac muscle. Tissues are made up of cells, which contain organelles like the mitochondria and the Golgi apparatus.

7.   Which of these is not a characteristic shared by all living things?

   A.   movement

   B.   made of cells

   C.   metabolism

   D.   reproduction

   E.   respond to stimuli

The answer is A.
Movement is not a characteristic of life. Viruses are considered non-living organisms but have the ability to move from cell to cell in its host organism. A leaf on a tree or the tree itself are very much alive but unable to move in terms of mobility.

8.   What is the purpose of the Golgi apparatus?

   A.   To break down proteins

   B.   To break down fats

   C.   To make carbohydrates.

   D.   To provide the cell with energy

   E.   To sort, modify and package molecules

The answer is E.
The Golgi apparatus takes molecules from the endoplasmic reticulum and sorts, modifies and packages the molecules for later use by the cell.

9.   **What do amyloplasts do?**

    A.   Store starch in a plant cell

    B.   Remove waste in animal cells

    C.   Produce green and yellow pigment

    D.   Aid in photosynthesis.

    E.   Provide energy for metabolism

The answer is A.
Amyloplasts store starch in plant cells

10.   **Which of the following does not belong to the domain Archaea?**

    A.   Methanogens

    B.   Extreme Halophiles

    C.   Thermoacidophiles

    D.   Bacteriophiles

    E.   Sulfobales

The answer is D.
The Archaea group includes all of the above except Bacteriophiles.

11.   The first cells that evolved on earth were probably of which type?

        A.   autotrophic

        B.   eukaryotic

        C.   heterotrophic

        D.   prokaryotic

        E.   endosymbiotic

The answer is D.
Prokaryotes date back to 3.5 billion years ago in the first fossil record. Their ability to adapt to the environment allows them to thrive in a wide variety of habitats.

12.   During which part of photosynthesis is oxygen given off?

        A.   light reactions

        B.   dark reactions

        C.   Krebs cycle

        D.   reduction of NAD+ to NADH

        E.   phosphorylation

The answer is A.
The conversion of solar energy to chemical energy occurs in the light reactions. Electrons are transferred by the absorption of light by chlorophyll and cause water to split, releasing oxygen as a waste product.

13. Bacteria commonly reproduce by a process called binary fission. Which of the following best defines this process?

   A. Viral vectors carry DNA to new bacteria.

   B. DNA from one bacterium enters another.

   C. DNA doubles and the bacterial cell divides.

   D. DNA from dead cells is absorbed into bacteria.

   E. Bacteria merge with others to form new species.

The answer is C.

Binary fission is the asexual process in which the bacteria divide in half after the DNA doubles. This results in an exact clone of the parent cell.

14. Which tool is best for studying the individual parts of cells?

   A. ultracentrifuge

   B. phase-contrast microscope

   C. CAT scan

   D. electron microscope

   E. light microscope

The answer is D.

The scanning electron microscope uses a beam of electrons to pass through the specimen. The resolution is about 1000 times greater than that of a light microscope. This allows the scientist to view extremely small objects, such as the individual parts of a cell.

15. **Which of these classifications includes the thermoacidophiles?**

    A. Plantae

    B. Animalia

    C. Bacteria

    D. Protista

    E. Archaea

The answer is E.
Thermoacidophiles, methanogens, and halobacteria are members of the Archaea group.

16. **Which of the following is not part of the cytoskeleton?**

    A. vacuoles

    B. microfilaments

    C. microtubules

    D. intermediate filaments

    E. motor proteins

The answer is A.
Vacuoles are mostly found in plants and hold stored food and pigments. The other three choices are fibers that make up the cytoskeleton found in both plant and animal cells.

17.   Of what are viruses made?

    A.   A protein coat surrounding a nucleic acid.

    B.   RNA and protein surrounded by a cell wall.

    C.   A nucleic acid surrounding a protein coat.

    D.   Protein surrounded by DNA.

    E. A lipid bilayer surrounding a protein coat and RNA.

The answer is A.
Viruses are composed of a protein coat surrounding a nucleic acid; either RNA or DNA.

18.   Which of these are used to classify protists into their major groups?

    A.   Their method of obtaining nutrition.

    B.   Their method of reproduction.

    C.   Their use of metabolism.

    D.   Their form and function.

    E. Their means of locomotion.

The answer is D.
The chaotic status of names and concepts of the higher classification of the protists reflects their great diversity in form, function, and life styles. The protists are often grouped as algae (plant-like), protozoa (animal-like), or fungus-like based on the similarity of their lifestyle and characteristics to these more defined groups.

19. Replication of chromosomes occurs during which phase of the cell cycle?

   A. prophase

   B. interphase

   C. metaphase

   D. anaphase

   E. metaphase

The answer is B.
Interphase is the stage where the cell grows and copies the chromosomes in preparation for the mitotic phase.

20. Which of these events occurs during telophase in a plant cell?

   A. the chromosomes are doubled

   B. a cell plate forms

   C. crossing over occurs

   D. a cleavage furrow develops

   E. spindle fibers become visible

The answer is B.
During plant cell telophase, a cell plate is observed whereas a cleavage furrow is formed in animal cells.

21.   What is the stage of mitosis seen in the diagram?

A.   anaphase

B.   metaphase

C.   telophase

D.   prophase

E.   interphase

The answer is B.

During metaphase, the centromeres are at opposite ends of the cell. Here the chromosomes are aligned with one another.

22.   **What is the stage of mitosis shown in the diagram?**

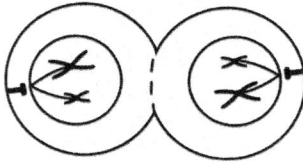

A.   prophase

B.   telophase

C.   anaphase

D.   metaphase

E.   interphase

The answer is B.

Telophase is the last stage of mitosis. Here, two nuclei become visible and the nuclear membrane reassembles.

23.   What is the stage of mitosis shown in the diagram?

A.   interphase

B.   metaphase

C.   prophase

D.   telophase

E.   anaphase

The answer is E.
During anaphase, the centromeres split in half and homologous chromosomes separate.

24.   Which of the following is a monomer?

A.   RNA

B.   glycogen

C.   DNA

D.   amino acid

E.   lipid

The answer is D.
A monomer is the simplest unit of structure for a particular macromolecule. Amino acids are the basic units that comprise a protein. RNA and DNA are polymers consisting of nucleotides and glycogen is a polymer consisting of many molecules of glucose.

25.   Which of the following does not affect enzyme rate?

    A.   increase of temperature

    B.   amount of substrate

    C.   pH

    D.   size of the cell

    E.   concentration of enzyme

The answer is D.
Temperature and pH can affect the rate of reaction of an enzyme. The amount of substrate affects the enzyme as well. The enzyme acts on the substrate. The more substrate, the slower the enzyme rate. Therefore, the only choice left is D, the size of the cell, which has no effect on enzyme rate.

26.   All but which one of the following is true of a cell membrane?

    A.   It contains polar and nonpolar phospholipids.

    B.   It only uses active transport to move molecules across it.

    C.   It contains cholesterol.

    D.   It has proteins imbedded within it.

    E.   It is selectively permeable to many substances.

The answer is B.
Cell membranes use passive and active transport to transport molecules across the membrane.

27. **Which of these describes facilitated diffusion?**

    A. It requires energy.

    B. It only happens in plant cells.

    C. It only allows molecules to leave a cell but not to enter it.

    D. It produces a significant amount of energy for the cell.

    E. It needs a transport molecule to pass through the membrane.

The answer is E.
Facilitated diffusion requires no energy but needs a transport molecule to pass another molecule through the membrane.

28. **What is not true of enzymes?**

    A. They are the most diverse of all proteins.

    B. They act on a substrate.

    C. They work at a wide range of pH.

    D. They are temperature-dependent.

    E. They have specialized functions.

The answer is C.
Enzymes generally work best within a very narrow range in pH.

29. Which of these is necessary for diffusion to occur?

    A. carrier proteins

    B. energy

    C. water molecules

    D. a cell membrane

    E. a concentration gradient

The answer is E.
Diffusion is the ability of molecules to move from areas of high concentration to areas of low concentration (a concentration gradient).

30. Which is an example of the use of energy to move a substance through a membrane from areas of low concentration to areas of high concentration?

    A. osmosis

    B. active transport

    C. exocytosis

    D. phagocytosis

    E. facilitated diffusion

The answer is B.
Active transport can move substances with or against the concentration gradient. This energy-requiring process allows for molecules to move from areas of low concentration to areas of high concentration.

31.   A plant cell is placed in salt water. What is the resulting movement of water out of the cell called?

    A.   facilitated diffusion

    B.   diffusion

    C.   transpiration

    D.   osmosis

    E.   active transport

The answer is D.
Osmosis is simply the diffusion of water across a semi-permeable membrane. Water will diffuse out of the cell if there is a lower concentration of water on the outside of the cell.

32.   What are the monomers of polysaccharides?

    A.   Nucleotides

    B.   Amino acids

    C.   Polypeptides

    D.   Fatty acids

    E.   Simple sugars

The answer is E.
The monomers of polysaccharides are simple sugars.

33.   Which type of cell would contain the most mitochondria?

A.   muscle cell

B.   nerve cell

C.   epithelial cell

D.   blood cell

E.   bone cell

The answer is A.
Mitochondria are the site of cellular respiration where ATP is made. Muscle cells have the most mitochondria because they use a great deal of energy.

34.   According to the fluid-mosaic model of the cell membrane, of what are membranes composed?

A.   Phospholipid bilayers with proteins embedded in the layers.

B.   One layer of phospholipids with cholesterol embedded in the layer.

C.   Two layers of protein with lipids embedded in the layers.

D.   DNA and fluid proteins with carbohydrates embedded in the layer.

E.   Glycerol and RNA with carbohydrates embedded in the layer.

The answer is A.
Cell membranes are composed of two phospholipids with their hydrophobic tails sandwiched between their hydrophilic heads, creating a lipid bilayer. The membrane contains proteins embedded in the layer (integral proteins) and proteins on the surface (peripheral proteins).

35. **Which is the correct statement regarding the human nervous system and the human endocrine system?**

   A. The nervous system maintains homeostasis whereas the endocrine system does not.

   B. Endocrine glands produce neurotransmitters whereas nerves produce hormones.

   C. Nerve signals travel on neurons whereas hormones travel through the blood.

   D. The nervous system involves chemical transmission whereas the endocrine system does not.

   E. The nervous system produces physiological responses whereas the endocrine produces behavioral.

The answer is C.
In the human nervous system, neurons carry nerve signals to and from the cell body. Endocrine glands produce hormones that are carried through the body in the bloodstream.

36. **Which process generates the most ATP?**

   A. fermentation

   B. glycolysis

   C. the Calvin cycle

   D. the Krebs cycle

   E. chemiosmosis

The answer is E.
The electron transport chain uses electrons to pump hydrogen ions across the mitochondrial membrane. This ion gradient is used to form ATP in a process called chemiosmosis. ATP is generated by the removal of hydrogen ions from NADH and $FADH_2$. This yields 34 ATP molecules.

37.   Which of these is a function of the cardiovascular system?

A.   Move oxygenated blood around the body

B.   Oxygenate the blood through gas exchange

C.   Act as an exocrine system

D.   Flush toxins out of the body

E.   Transport signals from the brain

The answer is A.
The cardiovascular system moves oxygenated blood around the body via the heart (a pump) and tubes (arteries and veins).

38.   Which of these is not a part of the nervous system?

A.   brain

B.   spinal cord

C.   axons

D.   venules

E.   cochlea

The answer is D.
Venules are part of the circulatory system. The others are part of the nervous system.

39.   Organisms need to maintain a constant internal environment to
        survive. Which of these is a method by which they achieve this?

        A.   respiration

        B.   reproduction

        C.   depolarization

        D.   repolarization

        E.   thermoregulation

The answer is E.
Thermoregulation is how an organism maintains its body temperature. If it is
an endothermic organism, it can respond to changes in temperature by
sweating or growing more fur. If it is an ectothermic organism, it can move to
a warmer or cooler location.

40.   Which of these controls the body's endocrine mechanisms?

        A.   feedback loops

        B.   control molecules

        C.   neurochemicals

        D.   neurotransmitters

        E.   behavioral responses

The answer is A.
The body's mechanisms are controlled by feedback loops.

41.   **What is the gland that regulates the calcium in the body?**

   A.   Thyroid gland

   B.   Parathyroid gland

   C.   Hypothalamus

   D.   Pituitary gland

   E.   Pancreas

The answer is B.
The parathyroid glands regulate the calcium levels in the body. They are imbedded within the thyroid gland.

42.   **Which of these steroids is not created in the gonads?**

   A.   Testosterone

   B.   Estrogen

   C.   Progesterone

   D.   ACTH

   E.   FSH

The answer is D.
ACTH is not one of the three steroids produced by the gonads. The other three are made by the gonads.

43.   **What is the most common neurotransmitter?**

  A.   epinephrine

  B.   serotonin

  C.   acetyl choline

  D.   norepinephrine

  E.   oxytocin

The answer is C.
The most common neurotransmitter is acetyl choline.

44.   **Food is carried through the digestive tract by a series of wave-like contractions. What is this process is called?**

  A.   peristalsis

  B.   chyme

  C.   digestion

  D.   absorption

  E.   depolarization

The answer is A.
Peristalsis is the process of wave-like contractions that moves food through the digestive tract.

45.   Which of these must muscles pull on in order to initiate movement?

A. skin

B. bones

C. joints

D. ligaments

E. bursa

The answer is B.
The muscular system's function is for movement. Skeletal muscles are attached to bones and are responsible for their movement.

46.   Hormones are essential to the regulation of reproduction. What organ is responsible for the release of hormones for sexual maturity?

A. pituitary gland

B. hypothalamus

C. pancreas

D. thyroid gland

E. pineal gland

The answer is B.
The hypothalamus begins secreting hormones that help mature the reproductive system and stimulate development of the secondary sex characteristics.

47. **What is the type of muscle in the human body that is voluntary?**

    A. Cardiac

    B. Sarcomere

    C. Smooth

    D. Skeletal

    E. Actin

The answer is D.
Of all of the above, only skeletal muscle is under voluntary control. It is found in the skeletal muscles of the human body.

48. **The wrist is an example of what kind of joint?**

    A. Ball and socket

    B. Pivot

    C. Stationary

    D. Hinge

    E. Gliding

The answer is B.
The wrist joint is a pivot joint.

49.   What is the waterproofing protein in the skin called?

  A.   actin

  B.   epidermis

  C.   collagen

  D.   sebum

  E.   keratin

The answer is E.
The waterproofing protein in the skin is called keratin.

50.   What is the muscular adaptation called that is used to move food through the digestive system?

  A.   peristalsis

  B.   passive transport

  C.   voluntary action

  D.   bulk transport

  E.   endocytosis

The answer is A.
Peristalsis is a process of wave-like contractions. This process allows food to be carried down the pharynx and though the digestive tract.

51.   **What is the role of neurotransmitters in nerve action?**

    A. to turn off the sodium pump

    B. to turn off the calcium pump

    C. to send impulses to neurons

    D. to send impulses around the body

    E. to send impulses from axon to dendrite

The answer is C.
The neurotransmitters carry the signals from one neuron to another across a gap called a synapse.

52.   **Fats are broken down by which substance?**

    A. bile produced in the gall bladder

    B. lipase produced in the gall bladder

    C. glucagons produced in the liver

    D. amylase produces in the gall bladder

    E. bile produced in the liver

The answer is E.
The liver produces bile, which breaks down and emulsifies fatty acids.

53.   Where does fertilization in humans usually occurs?

A.   uterus

B.   ovary

C.   fallopian tubes

D.   vagina

E.   epididymis

The answer is C.
Fertilization of the egg by the sperm normally occurs in the fallopian tube. The fertilized egg is then implanted on the uterine lining for development.

54.   Which of these is lacking in the dermis layer of skin?

A.   sweat glands

B.   keratin

C.   hair follicles

D.   blood vessels

E.   living cells

The answer is B.
Keratin is a water proofing protein found in the epidermis.

55. **A school age boy had the chicken pox as a baby. Why will he most likely not get this disease again?**

    A.   passive immunity

    B.   vaccination

    C.   antibiotics

    D.   active immunity

    E.   antigen production

The answer is D.
Active immunity develops after recovery from an infectious disease, such as the chicken pox, or after vaccination. Passive immunity to some diseases may be passed from one individual to another (from mother to nursing child).

56. **What is any foreign particle called that causes an immune reaction?**

    A.   an antigen

    B.   a histocompatibity complex

    C.   an antibody

    D.   a vaccine

    E.   a bacteriophage

The answer is A.
An antigen is any foreign particle that results in an immune reaction.

57.   Which of these statements describes the polymerase chain reaction?

    A.   It is a group of polymerases.

    B.   It is a technique for amplifying DNA.

    C.   It is a primer for DNA synthesis.

    D.   It is a way to synthesize polymerase.

    E.   It is a series of genetic mutations.

The answer is B.
PCR is a technique in which a piece of DNA can be amplified into billions of copies within a few hours.

58.   Which part of a DNA nucleotide can vary?

    A.   deoxyribose

    B.   phosphate group

    C.   hydrogen bonds

    D.   sugar

    E.   nitrogenous base

The answer is E.
DNA is made of a 5-carbon sugar (deoxyribose), a phosphate group, and a nitrogenous base. There are four nitrogenous bases in DNA that vary to allow for the four different nucleotides.

59.   A DNA strand has the base sequence of TCAGTA. Its DNA complement would have which of the following sequences?

    A. ATGACT

    B. TCAGTA

    C. AGUCAU

    D. AGTCAT

    E. TCTGTA

The answer is D.
The complement strand to a single strand DNA molecule has a complementary sequence to the template strand. T pairs with A and C pairs with G. Therefore, the complement to TCAGTA is AGTCAT.

60.   Which of these carries amino acids to the ribosome during protein synthesis?

    A. messenger RNA

    B. ribosomal RNA

    C. transfer RNA

    D. DNA

    E. RNA

The answer is C.
The tRNA molecule is specific for a particular amino acid. The tRNA has an anticodon sequence that is complementary to the codon. This specifies where the tRNA places the amino acid in protein synthesis.

61.   A protein is sixty amino acids in length. This requires a coded DNA
        sequence of how many nucleotides?

        A.   20

        B.   30

        C.   120

        D.   180

        E.   240

The answer is D.
Each amino acid codon consists of 3 nucleotides. If there are 60 amino acids
in a protein, then 60 x 3 = 180 nucleotides.

62.   A DNA molecule has the sequence of ACTATG. What is the
        anticodon of this molecule?

        A.   UGAUAC

        B.   ACTATG

        C.   TGATAC

        D.   ACUAUG

        E.   CTGCGA

The answer is D.
The DNA is first transcribed into mRNA. Here, the DNA has the sequence
ACTATG; therefore, the complementary mRNA sequence is UGAUAC
(remember, in RNA, T is U). This mRNA sequence is the codon. The
anticodon is the complement to the codon. The anticodon sequence will be
ACUAUG (remember, the anticodon is tRNA, so U is present instead of T).

63. **What is the general term for a change that affects the sequence of bases in a gene?**

    A. deletion

    B. polyploid

    C. mutation

    D. duplication

    E. substitution

The answer is C.
A mutation is an inheritable change in DNA. It may be an error in replication or a spontaneous rearrangement of one ore more segments of DNA. Deletion and duplication are types of mutations. Polyploidy is when an organism has more than two complete chromosome sets.

64. **Segments of DNA can be transferred from the DNA of one organism to another through the use of which of the following?**

    A. bacterial plasmids

    B. viruses

    C. chromosomes from frogs

    D. plant DNA

    E. Okazaki fragments

The answer is A.
Plasmids can transfer themselves (and therefore their genetic information) by a process called conjugation. This requires cell-to-cell contact.

65.   **What is the enzyme that unwinds DNA during replication?**

A.   DNAse

B.   DNA replicase

C.   DNA helicase

D.   DNA topoisomerases

E.   DNA polymerase

The answer is C.
The enzyme helicase is involved in unwinding DNA during replication.

66.   **What is a small circular piece of DNA called that contains accessory DNA?**

A.   mitochondrial DNA

B.   messenger RNA

C.   transfer DNA

D.   Okazaki fragment

E.   plasmid

The answer is E.
A plasmid is a small, circular piece of accessory DNA.

67.   In DNA, adenine bonds with _____, while cytosine bonds with
       _____.

       A.   thymine/guanine

       B.   adenine/cytosine

       C.   cytosine/uracil

       D.   guanine/thymine

       E.   uracil/adenine

The answer is A.
In DNA, adenine pairs with thymine and cytosine pairs with guanine
because of their nitrogenous base structures.

68.   **Which protein structure consists of the coils and folds of
       polypeptide chains?**

       A.   secondary structure

       B.   quaternary structure

       C.   tertiary structure

       D.   primary structure

       E.   quinary structure

The answer is A.
Primary structure is the protein's unique sequence of amino acids. Secondary
structure is the coils and folds of polypeptide chains. The coils and folds are
the result of hydrogen bonds along the polypeptide backbone. Tertiary
structure is formed by bonding between the side chains of the amino acids.
Quaternary structure is the overall structure of the protein from the
aggregation of two or more polypeptide chain

69. **What can be said about homozygous individuals?**

A. They have two different alleles.

B. They are of the same species.

C. They exhibit the same features.

D. They have a pair of identical alleles.

E. They produce identical offspring.

The answer is D.
Homozygous individuals have a pair of identical alleles and heterozygous individuals have two different alleles.

70. **The term "phenotype" refers to which of the following?**

A. a condition that is heterozygous

B. the genetic makeup of an individual

C. a condition that is homozygous

D. how the genotype is expressed

E. from which parent the traits were inherited

The answer is D.
Phenotype is the physical appearance or expression of an organism due to its genetic makeup (genotype).

71. The ratio of brown-eyed to blue-eyed children from the mating of a blue-eyed male to a heterozygous brown-eyed female is expected to be which of the following?

   A. 3:1

   B. 2:2

   C. 1:0

   D. 1:2

   E. 0:4

The answer is B.
Use a Punnet square to determine the ratio.

	b	b
B	Bb	Bb
b	bb	bb

B = brown eyes, b = blue eyes

Female genotype is on the side and the male genotype is across the top.

The female is heterozygous and her phenotype is brown eyes. This means the dominant allele is for brown eyes. The male expresses the homozygous recessive allele for blue eyes. Their children are expected to have a ratio of brown eyes to blue eyes of 2:2; or 1:1.

72.   Which of these defines the Law of Segregation defined by Gregor Mendel?

A.   After meiosis, each new cell will contain an allele that is recessive.

B.   Only one of two alleles is expressed in a heterozygous organism.

C.   The allele expressed is always the dominant allele.

D.   Alleles of one trait do not affect the inheritance of alleles on another chromosome.

E.   When sex cells form, the two alleles that determine a trait will end up on different gametes.

The answer is E.
The law of segregation states that the two alleles for each trait segregate into different gametes.

73.   Which of the following is an example of the incomplete dominance that occurs when a white flower is crossed with a red flower?

A.   pink flowers

B.   red flowers

C.   white flowers

D.   red and white flowers

E.   white and pink flowers

The answer is A.
Incomplete dominance is when the F_1 generation results in an appearance somewhere between the parents. Red flowers crossed with white flowers results in an F_1 generation with pink flowers.

74. A child with type O blood has a father with type A blood and a mother with type B blood. The genotypes of the parents respectively would be which of the following?

    A. AA and BO

    B. AO and BO

    C. AA and BB

    D. AO and OO

    E. OO and AB

The answer is B.
Type O blood has 2 recessive O genes. A child receives one allele from each parent; therefore, each parent in this example must have an O allele. The father has type A blood with a genotype of AO and the mother has type B blood with a genotype of BO.

75. Crossing over, which increases genetic diversity, occurs during which stage(s) of meiosis?

    A. telophase II in meiosis

    B. metaphase in mitosis

    C. interphase in meiosis

    D. prophase I in meiosis

    E. metaphase II in meiosis

The answer is D.
During prophase I of meiosis, the replicated chromosomes condense and pair with their homologues in a process called synapsis. Crossing over, the exchange of genetic material between homologues to further increase diversity, occurs during prophase I of meiosis.

76.   ABO blood grouping is an example of which type of allele
       dominance?

       A.   Autosomal dominance

       B.   Incomplete dominance

       C.   Somatic dominance

       D.   Complete dominance

       E.   Codominance

The answer is E.

ABO blood grouping involves codominance. This means that more than one
allele can express itself at the same time.

77.   In a Punnett square with a single trait, what are the ratios of
       genotypes produced between two heterozygous individuals?

       A.   1:2:2

       B.   2:1:1

       C.   1:1:1

       D.   1:2:1

       E.   2:2:2

The answer is D.

The Punnet square ratio for a single trait is 1:2:1. All three possible genotypes
will be expressed – homozygous dominant, heterozygous, and homozygous
recessive.

78.   **What is the term for an organism's genetic makeup?**

A.   Heterozygote

B.   Genotype

C.   Phenotype

D.   Homozygote

E.   Dominance

The answer is B.
The genetic makeup is called the genotype.

79.   **Which of these represents a genetic engineering advancement in the medical field?**

A.   stem cell reproduction

B.   pesticides

C.   degradation of harmful chemicals

D.   antibiotics

E.   gene therapy

The answer is E.
Gene therapy is the introduction of a normal allele to the somatic cells to replace a defective allele. The medical field has had success in treating patients with a single enzyme deficiency disease. Gene therapy has allowed doctors and scientists to introduce a normal allele that provides the missing enzyme.

80. **Which of the following is not true regarding restriction enzymes?**

    A. They aid in transcombination procedures.

    B. They are used in genetic engineering.

    C. They are named after the bacteria in which they naturally occur.

    D. They identify and splice certain base sequences on DNA.

    E. They can be produced by certain lipids during DNA replication.

The answer is A.
A restriction enzyme is a bacterial enzyme that cuts foreign DNA at specific locations. The splicing of restriction fragments into a plasmid results in a recombinant plasmid.

81. **Which of these processes is not one of the modern uses of DNA?**

    A. PCR technology

    B. Gene therapy

    C. Cloning

    D. Genetic Alignment

    E. Transgenic organisms

The answer is D.
PCR technology, gene therapy and cloning all come out of working with DNA.

82.   **Which statement best represents gel electrophoresis?**

   A.   It isolates fragments of DNA for scientific purposes.

   B.   It cannot be used in proteins.

   C.   It requires the polymerase chain reaction.

   D.   It only separates DNA by size.

   E.   It uses different charged particles to color the bands.

The answer is A.
Gel electrophoresis separates DNA by size and charge. It can be used in proteins as well and is not dependent on the polymerase chain reaction.

83.   **What is the term that describes the duplication of genetic material into another cell?**

   A.   replicating

   B.   cell duplication

   C.   transgenics

   D.   genetic restructuring

   E.   cloning

The answer is E.
Cloning is the duplication of genetic material into another cell.

84.   What does gel electrophoresis use to separate the DNA?

A.   the amount of current

B.   the size of the molecule

C.   the positive charge of the molecule

D.   the solubility of the gel

E.   the source of the DNA

The answer is B.
Electrophoresis uses electrical charges of molecules to separate them according to their size.

85.   Which of these is a result of reproductive isolation?

A.   extinction

B.   migration

C.   fossilization

D.   speciation

E.   radiation

The answer is D.
Reproductive isolation is caused by any factor that impedes two species from producing viable, fertile hybrids. Reproductive isolation of populations is the primary criterion for recognition of species status.

86.   Which of these is true about natural selection?

A.   It acts on an individual genotype.

B.   It is not currently happening.

C.   It is only an animal phenomenon.

D.   It acts on the individual phenotype.

E.   It is used to prevent overpopulation.

The answer is D.
Natural selection acts on the individual phenotype.

87.   How does diversity aid a population?

A. Individuals are better able to survive.

B.   Mates are attracted to a diverse population.

C. Potential mates like conformity.

D.   It increases the DNA differences in the population.

E.   It provides possible improvements to the population.

The answer is E.
Diversity provides possible improvements to the population.

88.   **Which statement is not true about diversity?**

        A.   Without diversity there would be extinction.

        B.   Diversity is increasing all the time.

        C.   Fossil evidence supports diversity.

        D.   Sexual reproduction encourages more diversity.

        E.   Skeletons are too similar to allow for diversity.

The answer is E.
The other answers are all true. Without diversity, there would be extinction, diversity is increasing all the time and fossil evidence supports an increase in diversity.

89.   **Which of these ideas was a major part of Darwin's evolutionary theory?**

        A.   Punctualism

        B.   Gradualism

        C.   Equilibrium

        D.   Convergency

        E.   Altruism

The answer is B.
Darwin's book is based upon gradualism, the idea that species change slowly over time.

90. **Which statement is not true about reproductive isolation?**

    A. It prevents populations from exchanging genes.

    B. It can occur by preventing fertilization.

    C. It can result in speciation.

    D. It happens more often on the mainland.

    E. It produces offspring with unique phenotypes

The answer is D.
Reproductive isolation can result in speciation, can occur by preventing fertilization and prevents populations from exchanging genes. It is a common phenomenon of islands.

91. **Which idea is true about members of the same species?**

    A. They look identical.

    B. They never change.

    C. They reproduce successfully within their group.

    D. They live in the same geographic location.

    E. They have very dissimilar genotypes.

The answer is C.
Species are defined by the ability to successfully reproduce with members of their own kind.

92. Which of the following factors will affect the Hardy-Weinberg law of equilibrium, leading to evolutionary change?

    A. no mutations

    B. non-random mating

    C. no immigration or emigration

    D. large population

    E. small individual species

The answer is B.
There are five requirements to keep the Hardy-Weinberg equilibrium stable: no mutation, no selection pressures, an isolated population, a large population, and random mating.

93. If a population is in Hardy-Weinberg equilibrium and the frequency of the recessive allele is 0.3, what percentage of the population is expected to be heterozygous?

    A. 9%

    B. 49%

    C. 42%

    D. 21%

    E. 7%

The answer is C.
0.3 is the value of q. Therefore, $q^2 = 0.09$. According to the Hardy-Weinberg equation, $1 = p + q$.
$1 = p + 0.3$.
$p = 0.7$
$p^2 = 0.49$ Next, plug q^2 and p^2 into the equation $1 = p^2 + 2pq + q^2$.
$1 = 0.49 + 2pq + 0.09$ (where 2pq is the number of heterozygotes).
$1 = 0.58 + 2pq$
$2pq = 0.42$ Multiply by 100 to get the percent of heterozygotes, 42%.

94. **Which aspect of science does not support evolution?**

    A. comparative anatomy

    B. organic chemistry

    C. comparison of DNA among organisms

    D. analogous structures

    E. embryology

The answer is B.
Comparative anatomy is the comparison of characteristics of the anatomies of different species. This includes homologous structures and analogous structures. The comparison of DNA between species is the best known way to place species on the evolution tree. Organic chemistry has nothing to do with evolution.

95. **In which of these does evolution occurs?**

    A. individuals

    B. populations

    C. organ systems

    D. cells

    E. ecosystems

The answer is B.
Evolution is a change in genotype over time. Gene frequencies shift and change from generation to generation. Populations evolve, not individuals.

96. Which process contributes most to the large variety of living things in the world today?

   A. meiosis

   B. asexual reproduction

   C. mitosis

   D. alternation of generations

   E. reproductive isolation

The answer is A.
During meiosis prophase I crossing over occurs. This exchange of genetic material between homologues increases diversity.

97. Which of the following gases was a major part of the primitive Earth atmosphere?

   A. fluorine

   B. methane

   C. oxygen

   D. krypton

   E. argon

The answer is B.
The primitive atmosphere contained ammonia, methane and hydrogen but very little oxygen.

98.   What is a major principle of the Endosymbiotic Theory?

    A.   Birds and dinosaurs share a common ancestor.

    B.   Animals evolved in close relationships with one another.

    C.   Prokaryotes arose from eukaryotes.

    D.   Inorganic compounds are the basis of living things.

    E.   Eukaryotes arose from very simple prokaryotes.

The answer is E.
The Endosymbiotic theory of the origin of eukaryotes states that eukaryotes arose from symbiotic groups of prokaryotic cells. According to this theory, smaller prokaryotes lived within larger prokaryotic cells, eventually evolving into chloroplasts and mitochondria.

99.   **The wing of a bird, the human arm, and the pectoral fluke of a whale all have the same bone structure. What are these structures called?**

    A.   polymorphic structures

    B.   homologous structures

    C.   vestigial structures

    D.   analogous structures

    E.   allopatric structures

The answer is B.
Homologous structures have the same genetic basis (leading to similar appearances), but are used for different functions.

100. Which of the following is not an abiotic factor?

 A. temperature

 B. rainfall

 C. soil quality

 D. predation

 E. wind speed

The answer is D.
Abiotic factors are non-living aspects of an ecosystem. Temperature, rainfall, and soil quality are all abiotic factors. Predation is an example of a biotic factor-- living things.

101. What is not true about cladistics?

 A. It is the study of phylogenetic relationships of organisms.

 B. It involves a branching diagram that uses the development of novel traits to separate groups of organisms.

 C. It distinguishes between the relative importance of the traits.

 D. It shows when traits developed with respect to other traits.

 E. It indicates which organisms are most closely related to each other and what their common ancestors were.

The answer is C.
Cladistics does not show how important certain traits were to different species. It represents when species evolved and how closely related they are to each other.

102.   If DDT were present in an ecosystem, which of the following organisms would have the highest concentration in its body?

A.   herring

B.   diatom

C.   zooplankton

D.   salmon

E.   osprey

The answer is E.
Chemicals and pesticides accumulate along the food chain. Tertiary consumers have more accumulated toxins than animals at the bottom of the food chain.

103.   What eats secondary consumers?

A.   Producers

B.   Tertiary consumers

C.   Primary consumers

D.   Decomposers

E.   Detritivores

The answer is B.
The tertiary consumers eat the secondary consumers and the secondary consumers eat the primary consumers.

104.   Which statement is true about the water cycle?

A.   Two percent of the water is fixed and unavailable.

B.   75% of available water is groundwater.

C.   The water cycle is driven by the ocean currents.

D.   Surface water percolates up from underground springs.

E.   New water is being added into the cycle all the time.

The answer is A.

96 percent of available water is groundwater. The water cycle is driven by the sun. Surface water is available.

105.   Which statement about the carbon cycle is false?

A.   Ten percent of all available carbon is in the air.

B.   Carbon dioxide is fixed by glycosylation.

C.   Plants fix carbon in the form of glucose.

D.   Animals release carbon through respiration.

E.   Most atmospheric carbon comes from the decay of dead organisms.

The answer is B.

Ten percent of all available carbon is in the air. Plants fix carbon via photosynthesis to make glucose and animals release carbon through respiration.

106. **What is the impact of sulfur oxides and nitrogen oxides in the environment when they react with water?**

   A.   ammonia

   B.   acidic precipitation

   C.   sulfuric acid

   D.   global warming

   E.   greenhouse effect

The answer is B.
Acidic precipitation is rain, snow, or fog with a pH less than 5.6. It is caused by sulfur oxides and nitrogen oxides that react with water in the air to form acids that fall down to Earth as precipitation.

107. **Which term is not associated with the water cycle?**

   A.   precipitation

   B.   transpiration

   C.   fixation

   D.   evaporation

   E.   runoff

The answer is C.
Water is recycled through the processes of evaporation and precipitation. Transpiration is the evaporation of water from leaves. Fixation is not associated with the water cycle.

108.   Which of the following is a density dependent factor that affects a
        population?

    A.   temperature

    B.   rainfall

    C.   predation

    D.   soil nutrients

    E.   wind speed

The answer is C.
As a population increases, the competition for resources is intense and the
growth rate declines. This is a density-dependent factor. An example of this
would be predation. Density-independent factors affect the population
regardless of its size. Examples of density-independent factors are rainfall,
temperature, and soil nutrients.

109.   High humidity and temperature stability are present in which of the
        following biomes?

    A.   taiga

    B.   deciduous forest

    C.   desert

    D.   tropical rain forest

    E.   coniferous forest

The answer is D.
A tropical rain forest is located near the equator. Its temperature is at a
constant 25 degrees C and the humidity is high due to the rainfall that
exceeds 200 cm per year.

110. Which trophic level has the highest ecological efficiency?

   A. decomposers

   B. producers

   C. tertiary consumers

   D. secondary consumers

   E. primary consumers

The answer is B.
The amount of energy that is transferred between trophic levels is called the ecological efficiency. The visual of this is represented in a pyramid of productivity. The producers have the greatest amount of energy and are at the bottom of this pyramid.

111. From where does the oxygen created in photosynthesis come?

   A. carbon dioxide

   B. chlorophyll

   C. glucose

   D. carbon monoxide

   E. water

The answer is E.
In photosynthesis, water is split; the hydrogen atoms are pulled to carbon dioxide that is taken in by the plant and ultimately reduced to make glucose. The oxygen from the water is given off as a waste product.

112. Which of the following is true of decomposers?

A. Decomposers recycle the carbon accumulated in durable organic material.

B. They take nitrogen out of the soil to use for food.

C. Decomposers absorb nutrients from the air to maintain their metabolisms.

D. Decomposers belong to the Genus *Escherichia*.

E. They are able to use the Sun to produce their own energy.

The answer is A.
Decomposers recycle phosphorus and carbon and undergo ammonification. The break down dead organisms to release the carbon held within their tissues. This carbon then reenters the ecosystem.

113. A clownfish is protected by a sea anemone's tentacles, and in turn, the anemone receives uneaten food from the clownfish. What type of symbiosis is exemplified by this example?

A. mutualism

B. parasitism

C. commensalism

D. competition

E. amensalism

The answer is A.
Neither the clownfish nor the anemone cause harmful effects towards one another and they both benefit from their relationship. Mutualism is when two species that occupy a similar space benefit from their relationship.

114.   Which of these is most likely to happen in order for primary succession to occur?

   A.   nutrient enrichment

   B.   a forest fire

   C.   bare rock is exposed after a water table recedes

   D.   a housing development is built

   E.   a farmer stops cultivating her fields

The answer is C.
Primary succession occurs where life never existed before, such as flooded areas or a new volcanic island. It is only after the water recedes that the rock is able to support new life.

115.   What is the Mendelian law called that states that only one of the two possible alleles from each parent is passed on to the offspring?

   A.   The Mendelian Law

   B.   The Law of Independent Assortment

   C.   The Law of Segregation

   D.   The Allele Law

   E.   The Law of Dominance and Recessiveness

The answer is B.
The law of independent assortment states that only one of a pair of alleles is transferred from parent to offspring.

Description of the Examination

The CLEP College Composition examinations assess writing skills taught in most first-year college composition courses. Those skills include analysis, argumentation, synthesis, usage, ability to recognize logical development and research. The exams cannot cover every skill (such as keeping a journal or peer editing) required in many first-year college writing courses. Candidates will, however, be expected to apply the principles and conventions used in longer writing projects to two timed writing assignments and to apply the rules of standard written English.

College Composition contains approximately 50 multiple-choice items to be answered in approximately 50 minutes and two essays to be written in 70 minutes (with 30 minutes to write the first essay and 40 minutes to read the two sources and write the second essay), for a total of approximately 120 minutes testing time. Essays must be typed on the computer.

The actual examination contains multiple-choice items and two mandatory, centrally scored essays. The essays are scored twice a month by college English faculty from throughout the country via an online scoring system. Each of the two essays is scored independently by two different readers, and the scores are then combined. This combined score is weighted approximately equally with the score from the multiple-choice section. These scores are then combined to yield the candidate's score. The resulting combined score is reported as a single score between 20 and 80. Separate scores are not reported for the multiple-choice and essay sections.

Knowledge and Skills

The subject matter of the College Composition examination is drawn from the following topics. The percentages next to the main topics indicate the approximate percentage of exam questions on that topic for the 50 multiple-choice items.

10%   Conventions of Standard English
- measures the awareness of logical, structural and grammatical relationships within sentences. Questions relate to syntax, punctuation, concord/agree

ment, modifiers,
active versus
passive voice and
additional areas

40% **Revision Skills**
- measures revision
  skills in the context
  of early essays, such
  as organization,
  level of detail,
  awareness of
  audience or tone,
  sentence variety and
  structure, main
  ideas, transitions,
  point of views

25% **Ability to Use Source Material**
- measures familiarity
  with basic reference
  and research skills
  via the use of
  reference materials,
  evaluation of
  sources, integration
  of resources and
  documentation

25% **Rhetorical Analysis**
- measures ability to
  analyze writing
  primarily using
  passage based
  questions reviewing
  appeals, tone,
  structure, rhetorical
  effects

<u>SAMPLE TEST</u>

There are 50 questions that you must answer in less than 50 minutes. Then, there are essay questions that you must answer in a timed fashion: the first essay has 30 minutes and the second essay has 40 minutes to read two passages and complete and essay.

Remember, your goals for this test are those questions you answer accurately; it is not based on how many are incorrect. Take your time, and good luck.

DIRECTIONS: Read each item carefully, paying attention to the underlined portions. If there is an error, it will be underlined. Assume that elements of the sentence not underlined are correct. If there is an error, select the one underlined part and enter that letter on the answer sheet. If there is no error, choose E

1. On a long day in October, the rain <u>fell</u> so hard that it <u>causes</u> flooding all <u>along</u> the highway, <u>bringing</u> traffic to a stop. <u>No error.</u>

   A. fell

   B. causes

   C. along

   D. bringing

   E. No error

2. <u>Their</u> attempts are almost always comical, not <u>being able</u> to move supplies without <u>loosing</u> at least one package on the <u>route</u>. <u>No error.</u>

   A. Their

   B. being able

   C. loosing

   D. route

   E. No error

3. At least two of the seven <u>defendents</u> <u>want</u> a delay, <u>saying</u> they need more time <u>to prepare</u> for trial. <u>No error.</u>

A. defendents

B. want

C. saying

D. to prepare

E. No eror

4. The surfer <u>was bit</u> by a shark, but <u>got</u> his revenge when he <u>caught</u> him and <u>ate</u> it for dinner. <u>No error</u>

A. was bit

B. got

C. caught

D. ate

E. No error

5. A portrait of a <u>women</u> <u>had been</u> painted onto an iceberg, which was precariously <u>perched</u> on the edge of a melting <u>piece</u> of glacier. <u>No error</u>

A. women

B. had been

C. perched

D. piece

E. No error

Read the following paragraph and answer the questions that follow.

There was a steaming mist in all the hollows, and it roamed in its forlornness up the hill, like an evil spirit, seeking rest and finding none. A clammy and intensely cold mist, it made its way through the air in ripples that visibly followed and overspread one another, as the waves of an unwholesome sea might do. It was dense enough to shut out everything from the light of the coach-lamps but these its own workings, and a few yards of road; and the reek of the laboring horses steamed into it, as if they had made it at all.

211

6. The description of this scene gives the impression that it is:

A. an oppressive journey.

B. an enlightening route.

C. a contemplative traveling discussion.

D. an entertaining troupe making way to the next show.

E. None of these things is true.

7. What is the main idea of this passage?

A. Weather sets the stage in any narrative.

B. The coach horses were not up to the task of the road.

C. It was a dark and cold night, relatively unsuitable for travel.

D. One of the coach-lamps was unlit, making it difficult to see.

E. An English countryside scene is perfect for a scary setting.

8. The author's purpose is to:

A. Inform

B. Entertain

C. Persuade

D. Narrate

E. Analyze

Read the following passage and answer the questions that follow.

Everyone called him Pop Eye. Even in those days when I was a skinny thirteen-year-old I thought he probably knew about his nickname but didn't care. His eyes were too interested in what lay up ahead to notice us barefoot kids.

He looked like someone who had seen or known great suffering and hadn't been able to forget it. His large eyes in his large head stuck out further than anyone else's - like they wanted to lave the surface of his face. They made you think of someone who can't get out the house quickly enough.

Pop Eye wore the same white linen suit every day.

His trousers snagged onto hi sony knees in the sloppy heat. Some days he wore a clown's nose. His nose was already big. he didn't need that red light bulb. But for reasons we couldn't think of he wore the red nose on certain days that may have meant something to him. We never saw him smile. And on those days he wore the clowns nose you found yourself looking away because you never saw such sadness.

9. **What is the main idea of the passage?**

   A. The main character was a generally sad man, disinterested in the scene around him.

   B. The main character cannot remember the thirteen-year-old kid.

   C. The physical appearance of the main character was awkward.

   D. The main character was so poor that he only had one suit.

   E. None of these represent the main idea of the passage.

10. **From the passage, one can infer that:**

    A. Pop Eye is surrounded by family.

    B. Pop Eye works as a clown.

    C. The narrator is related to Pop Eye.

    D. Pop Eye lives a lonely life.

    E. The narrator has done well for himself.

11. **What is the author's purpose in writing this passage?**

    A. To entertain

    B. To narrate

    C. To describe

    D. To persuade

    E. To make demands

12. The author implies that :

A. the main character had secret talents.

B. the main character had great sadness.

C. the narrator was related to the main character.

D. the main character was generally neat and tidy.

E. the narrator was homeless.

Read the following passage excerpted from Biography.com and choose the best answer to the questions that follow.

A prolific artist, Austrian composer Wolfgang Mozart created a string of operas, concertos, symphonies and sonatas that profoundly shaped classical music. Over the years, Mozart aligned himself with a variety of European venues and patrons, composing hundreds of works that included sonatas, symphonies, masses, concertos and operas, marked by vivid emotion and sophisticated textures.

During the time when he worked for Archbishop Hieronymus von Colleredo, young Mozart had the opportunity to work in several different musical genres composing symphonies, string quartets, sonatas and serenades and a few operas. He developed a passion for violin concertos producing what came to be the only five he wrote.

In 1776, he turned his efforts toward piano concertos, culminating in the Piano Concerto Number 9 in E flat major in early 1777. In Salzburg in 1779, Wolfgang Amadeus Mozart produced a series of church works, including the Coronation Mass. He also composed another opera for Munich, Ideomeneo in 1781.

13. Who is the target audience of this passage?

A. Artists.

B. Austrians.

C. Catholics.

D. A person interested in classical music.

E. None of these are accurate.

214

14. **What is the main idea of the previous passage?**

   A. Mozart had a sister that also performed with him.

   B. Mozart's father was his promoter.

   C. The Catholic church was supportive of Mozart's talent.

   D. Many operas and other pieces were composed by Mozart before he was 25 years old.

   E. The rapid development and appreciation of Mozart's music.

15. **What is the author's purpose in writing this?**

   A. To describe

   B. To narrate

   C. To entertain

   D. To inform

   E. To argue

16. **From reading this passage, we can conclude that:**

   A. Mozart wrote several complex pieces of music at a young age.

   B. There were not many composers as young and talented as Mozart.

   C. There was a special relationship between the Catholic church and Mozart's family.

   D. There were not as many composers in Austria as other countries.

   E. None of these are accurate.

17. Which of the following is not a musical genre?

A. Opera

B. Sonnet

C. Symphony.

D. Concerto.

E. Quartet.

Read the following paragraph and answer the questions that follow.

(1)Outside, the late afternoon sun slanted down in the yard, throwing into gleaming brightness the dogwood trees that were solid masses of white blossoms against the background of new green. (2)The twins' horses were hitched in the driveway, big animals, red as their masters' hair; and around the horses' legs quarreled the pack of lean, nervous possum hounds that accompanied Stuart and Brent wherever they went. (3)A little aloof, as became and aristocrat, lay a black-spotted carriage dog, puzzle on paws, patiently waiting for the boys to go home to supper.

18. What is the main idea of this passage?

A. The passage is describing an afternoon outdoor setting.

B. The twins had very poised animals.

C. Certain concessions should be made for dogs.

D. The difficulties of travel in thick blossoming forests.

E. None of these covey the main idea of the passage.

19. What is the author's main purpose?

A. To inform

B. To entertain

C. To describe

D. To narrate

E. To record

20. What type of sentence is the second sentence?

A. Simple

B. Compound

C. Complex

D. Complex-Compound

E. Dependent clause

Read the following paragraph from Wikipedia and answer the question that follows.

Isaac Newton built the first practical reflecting telescope and developed a theory of colour based on the observation that a prism decomposes white light into the many colors of the visible spectrum. He formulated an empirical law of cooling, studied the speed of sound, and introduced the notion of a Newtonian fluid. In addition to his work on calculus, as a mathematician Newton contributed to the study of power series, generalized the binomial theorem to non-integer exponents, developed a method for approximating the roots of a function, and classified most of the cubic plane curves.

21. What is the main idea of this passage?

A. Power series is an important part of scientific discovery.

B. Fluid engineering is about the empirical law of cooling.

C. Through telescopes, scientists have made discoveries that have helped many people.

D. Newton was a mathematician and a scientist.

E. None of the above.

Read the following paragraph from *Popular Mechanics* and answer the question that follows.

We've been finding planets beyond our solar system for two decades now, but there are good reasons why it's taken so long to find the first forming world. For one thing, Stephanie Sallum says, planets spend only a brief period of their long lives in formation. Simply looking at the the odds, "it's

unlikely that you'll come across a planet when it's still forming," she says.

22. The author's purpose is to

    A. Describe

    B. Inform

    C. Persuade

    D. Narrate

    E. Summarize

Read the following paragraph from National Geographic and answer the question.

So far, more than 150 countries – from Sudan to Suriname and from Kiribati to Kyrgyzstan – have outlined for United Nations negotiators just how, when, and by how much each would cut carbon dioxide over the next several decades. If an agreement is reached, it would mark the first serious global commitment to reduce the pollution that is warming the planet, souring the oceans, and causing seas to rise.

23. What type of organizational pattern is the author using?

    A. Comparison and Contrast

    B. Generalization

    C. Cause and Effect

    D. Simple Listing

    E. Analogy

Read the following paragraph from *Antiques and Fine Art* and answer the following question.

Since the colonial period, the Atlantic Ocean has operated both as a barrier between America and Europe and as a conduit for international exchanges of peoples, goods, and ideas. It spurred commerce and enterprise that was the basis for both national economic activity and personal fortune. The activities in America's great harbors and port cities also supported the nation's cultural development, prompting the rise of schools of maritime and landscape painting, as well as portraiture.

24. Which organizational pattern does the author use?

    A. Comparison and Contrast

    B. Simple Listing

    C. Cause and Effect

    D. Definition

    E. Description

Read the following quote and answer the following question.

"I don't think about whether people will remember me or not. I've been an okay person. I've learned a lot. I've taught people a thing or two. That's what's important." – Julia Child

25. The quote primarily:

    A. describes.

    B. informs.

    C. entertains.

    D. narrates.

    E. lists.

26. Addressing someone absent or something inhuman as though present and able to respond describes a figure of speech known as:

    A. personification

    B. synecdoche

    C. metonymy

    D. apostrophe

    E. rhetorical strategy

Read the following paragraphs and answer the questions that follows.

A. At the end of the period, the artistic temperament of the painter undergoes a profound modification; it reflects a set of assimilated romantic ideas, expands the grandeur of classical art, and, while in the early works the love for the antique style throughout the popular subjects with inanimate edifice with the classic treatment as well as characterless, mythological subjects in the frescoes. The painter's figures assume heroic proportions, exude solemn expressions, and everything seems to come alive in a life more lush, more monumental and simple at the same time...

B. Overall, we find an artist's determined personality, animated by a continuous and rapid progress, the result of a clear conscience and scrupulous study fiery aspects of reality with which can be sympathized, of an intense search of technical development, the assimilation of many and beautiful expressions of art. So he states, from the beginning of his artistic activity, a teacher of exceptional importance, which rises with noble means and personal and solid, without resorting to defiant rage, the glitz, the stylism that characterize so remarkable part of the art of his time.

C. Serra, Luigi. Domenico Zampieri detto Il Domenichino. Rome: Casa Editrice del Bollettino d'Arte, Del Ministero Della P. Istruzione. 1909. pp11-12.

27. Where does the excerpt originate?

A. Webster's Dictionary

B. Luigi Serra

C. Domenico Zampieri

D. World Book Encyclopedia

E. Wikipedia

28. In the second paragraph, the second sentence can best be described as:

A. compound.

B. complex.

C. run-on.

D. a fragment.

E. compound-complex.

29. This, H. (2006). Food for Tomorrow? How the Scientific Discipline of Molecular Gastronomy Could Change the Way We Eat. *EMBO Reports,* 7(11), 1062-1066.

In the citation, 1062 provides what information?

A. Date printed

B. Date accessed

C. First page of reference

D. Last page of reference

E. None of these are correct

30. In the citation above, the (11) refers to:

A. the eleventh article in the magazine.

B. the eleventh article published by this author.

C. there are eleven articles on gastronomy in this issue.

D. there are eleven authors.

E. This is the eleventh issue in the series, in volume seven.

31. In the *EMBO* citation above, 7 refers to what?

A. The number of volumes this has magazine has published in 2006.

B. How many articles have discussed gastronomy in the magazine's history

C. The seventh report for this issue.

D. Pagination.

E. Tagnemics

32. Bernstein, M. (2002). 10 tips on writing the living Web. *A List Apart: For People Who Make Websites, 149.* Retrieved from http://www.alistapart.com/articles/writeliving is a citation example of a:

A. newspaper.

B. book.

C. online periodical.

D. abstract.

E. none of these selections are accurate.

33. 2. Weinstein, "Plato's *Republic,*" 452–53.

This is an example of:

A. note style.

B. duplicate style.

C. bibliography.

D. APA style.

E. MLA style.

34. Kossinets, Gueorgi, and Duncan J. Watts. "Origins of Homophily in an Evolving Social Network." *American Journal of Sociology* 115 (2009): 405–50. Accessed February 28, 2010. doi:10.1086/599247.

Which style is this?

A. MLA

B. APA

C. Chicago

D. New York

E. None of these

35. Maxmen, Amy. "How Ebola Found Fertile Ground in Sierra Leone's Chaotic Capital." National Geographic. 27 January, 2015. Web. 16 November, 2015.

This is an example of what kind of citation format?

A. MLA

B. APA

C. Chicago

D. Turabian

E. None of these

36. In the citation above, what does 27 January 2015 reference?

A. Reference date

B. Publication date

C. Editing date

D. Web upload date

E. None of these

37. Treverton, Gregory F. "The Changed Target." *Intelligence for an Age of Terror.* Cambridge: Cambridge UP, 2009. 24-25. Print. What does print reference?

A. Magazine article

B. Newspaper article

C. Printed web source

D. Book

E. None of these

Read the following paragraph from the *National Independent Schools Magazine* and answer the questions that follow.

The bias against introverted students is embedded in our educational system: years of unrelenting focus on cooperative learning, thinking aloud, and talking-as-learning, with grades for class participation, required public speaking (often now as a disproportionate pedagogical focus displacing more traditional forms of scholarship and substantive mastery), and a pervasive, almost normative, value placed on being social and well liked, particularly in a large-group context. In sum, the classroom focus is now too often on "doing," in sacrifice to "thinking."

38. **What is meant by the word "un- relenting" in the first sentence?**

   A. Continuing

   B. Protective

   C. Pervasive

   D. Cautious

   E. Reckless

39. **What is the author's tone?**

   A. Aseptic

   B. Analytical

   C. Disbelieving

   D. Disapproving

   E. Scornful

40. **What type of organizational pattern is the author using?**

   A. Classification

   B. Explanation

   C. Comparison and Contrast

   D. Cause and Effect

   E. Entertaining

41. Who would be the intended audience of this excerpt?

   A. Politicians, for funding purposes.

   B. Social workers, for counseling purposes.

   C. Teachers, for refocusing efforts.

   D. Parents, for normative adjustments.

   E. None of these are applicable.

Read the following passage from Roll of Thunder, Hear My Cry and answer the questions that follow.

My youngest brother paid no attention to me. Grasping more firmly his newspaper-wrapped notebook and his tin-can lunch of cornbread and oil sausages, he continued to concentrate on the dusty road. He lagged several feet behind my other brothers, Stacey and Christopher-John, and me, attempting to keep the rusty Mississippi dust from swelling with each step and drifting back upon his shiny black shoes and the cuffs of his corduroy pants by lifting each foot high before setting it gently down again. Always meticulously neat, six-year-old Little Man never allowed dirt or tears or stains to mar anything he owned. Today was no exception.

"You keep it up and make us late for school, Mama's gonna wear you out," I threatened, pulling with exasperation at the high collar of the Sunday dress Mama had made me wear for the first day of school - as if that event were something special. It seemed to me that showing up at school all on a bright August-like October morning made for running the cool forest trails and wading barefoot in the forest pond was concession enough; Sunday clothing was asking too much. Christopher-John and Stacey were not too pleased about the clothing or school either. Only Little Man, just beginning his school career, found the prospects of both intriguing.

42. What is the meaning of the word "meticulously" in the next to last sentence in the first paragraph?

    A. Many

    B. Very

    C. Exceptionally

    D. Rarely

    E. Fairly

43. What is the overall organizational pattern used in this passage?

    A. Generalization

    B. Cause and Effect

    C. Addition

    D. Descriptive

    E. Informational

44. What is the author's tone?

    A. Disbelieving

    B. Exasperated

    C. Informative

    D. Optimistic

    E. None of these are correct.

Read the following passage from Pride and Prejudice and answer the questions that follow.

Mr. Bennet was so odd a mixture of quick parts, sarcastic humour, reserve, and caprice, that the experience of three-and-twenty years had been insufficient to make his wife understand his character. Her mind was less difficult to develop. She was a woman of mean understanding, little information, and uncertain temper. When she was discontented, she fancied herself nervous. The business of her life was to get her daughters married; its solace was visiting and news.

Mr. Bennet was among the earliest of those who waited on Mr. Bingley. He had always intended to visit him, though to the last always assuring his wife that he should not go; and till the evening after the visit was paid she had no knowledge of it. It was then disclosed in the following manner. Observing his second daughter employed in trimming a hat, he suddenly addressed her with:

"I hope Mr. Bingley will like it, Lizzy."

45. What is the overall organizational pattern of this passage?

   A. Generalization

   B. Cause and Effect

   C. Addition

   D. Summary

   E. Informational

46. What is the meaning of the phrase "uncertain temper" in the third sentence?

   A. Hot tempered

   B. Quixotic emotions

   C. Unusually morose

   D. Generally happy

   E. None of these apply

47. What is the organizational pattern of the second paragraph?

   A. Cause and Effect

   B. Classification

   C. Addition

   D. Explanation

   E. None of these things

Read the following passage from Wuthering Heights and answer the questions that follow.

Before passing the threshold, I pause to admire a quantity of grotesque carving lavished over the front, and especially about the principal door; above which, among a wilderness of crumbling griffins and shameless little boys, I detected the date '1500,' and the name 'Hareton Earnshaw.' I would have made a few comments, and requested a short history of the plane from the surly owner; but his attitude at the door appeared to demand my speedy entrance, or complete departure, and I had no desire to aggregate his impatience previous to inspecting the penetralium.

48. What is the author's overall organizational pattern?

 A. Classification

 B. Cause and Effect

 C. Definition

 D. Comparison and Contrast

 E. None of these things

49. The author's tone in the passage is one of:

 A. Inquisition

 B. Excitement

 C. Surliness

 D. Concern

 E. Impatience

50. The most similar way to rephrase "I had no desire to aggregate his impatience" in context of the passage would be:

 A. I wanted to keep him happy

 B. I didn't want to make him mad

 C. I didn't want to stay around

 D. I wanted him to quickly inspect the penetralium

 E. None of these are approximations

SAMPLE TEST ESSAY 1

As a reminder, you have 30 minutes to compose your essay and type it on the computer.

Directions: Write an essay in which you discuss the extent to which you agree or disagree with the statement below. Support your discussion with specific reasons and examples from your reading, experience or observations.

Topic: *Beauty is in the eye of the beholder.*

Readers will assign scores based on a matrix, or scoring guide. Here is an example outline of how both student essays will be graded on a six point scale.

SCORE OF 6 - The 6 essay presents a thesis that is coherent and well-developed. The writer's ideas are detailed, intelligent, and thoroughly elaborated. The writer's use of language and structure is correct and meaningful.

SCORE OF 5 - The 5 essay presents a thesis and offers persuasive support. The writer's ideas are usually new, mature, and thoroughly developed. A command of language and a variety of structures are evident.

SCORE OF 4 - The 4 essay presents a thesis and frequently offers a plan of development, which is usually demonstrated. The writer offers sufficient details to achieve the purpose of the essay. There is capable use of language and varied sentence structure. Errors in sentence structure and usage don't interfere with the writer's main purpose.

SCORE OF 3 - The 3 essay gives a thesis and offers a plan of development, which is usually demonstrated. The writer gives support that leans toward generalized statements or a listing. Overall, the support in a 3 essay is neither adequate nor coherent enough to be convincing. There are errors in sentence structure and usage that frequently interfere with the writer's ability to state the purpose.

SCORE OF 2 - The 2 essay usually states a thesis. The writer offers support that may be incomplete. Simple and disconnected sentence structure is present. Mistakes in grammar and usage often thwart the writer's ability to state the purpose.

SCORE OF 1 - The 1 essay has a thesis that is pointless or poorly articulated. Support is shallow. The language is muddled and confusing. Many mistakes in grammar and usage.

SAMPLE ESSAY 2

As a reminder, you have 40 minutes to read these two passages and type your essay on the computer.

Directions: Write an essay in which you incorporate the two sources of information provided below. You must use both sources and you must use appropriate citation for both sources using the author's last name, the title or by any other means that adequately identifies it. Support your discussion with specific reasons and examples from your reading, experience or observations.

Assignment: Read the following sources carefully. Then write an essay in which you develop a position on whether people or communities express devotion differently.

Introduction: Devotion, according to Oxford's Dictionary, is "love, loyalty or enthusiasm for a person, activity, or cause."

Source 1: Shakespeare, William. *Romeo and Juliet.* England: 1595.

"But, soft! what light through yonder window breaks?
It is the east, and Juliet is the sun.
Arise, fair sun, and kill the envious moon,
Who is already sick and pale with grief,
That thou, her maid, art far more fair than she.
Be not her maid, since she is envious;
Her vestal livery is but sick and green
And none but fools do wear it; cast it off.
It is my lady, O, it is my love!
Oh, that she knew she were!"

Source 2: Heller, Joseph. "Catch 22." United States: 1961.

"What is a country? A country is a piece of land surrounded on all sides by boundaries, usually unnatural."

ANSWER KEY

Question Number	Correct Answer	Your Answer	Question Number	Correct Answer	Your Answer
1	B		26	A	
2	C		27	B	
3	A		28	C	
4	A		29	C	
5	A		30	E	
6	A		31	A	
7	C		32	C	
8	D		33	B	
9	A		34	C	
10	D		35	A	
11	C		36	B	
12	B		37	D	
13	D		38	A	
14	E		39	D	
15	D		40	D	
16	A		41	C	
17	B		42	C	
18	A		43	D	
19	C		44	B	
20	D		45	A	
21	D		46	B	
22	B		47	D	
23	C		48	E	
24	A		49	A	
25	B		50	B	

RATIONALES

CONVENTIONS OF STANDARD WRITTEN ENGLISH

DIRECTIONS: Read each item carefully, paying attention to the underlined portions. If there is an error, it will be underlined. Assume that elements of the sentence not underlined are correct. If there is an error, select the one underlined part and enter that letter on the answer sheet. If there is no error, choose E.

1. On a long day in October, the rain <u>fell</u> so hard that it <u>causes</u> flooding all <u>along</u> the highway, <u>bringing</u> traffic to a stop. <u>No error.</u>

    A. fell

    B. causes

    C. along

    D. bringing

    E. No error

The answer is B.
Causes should be caused, as the sentence is written in the past tense.

2. <u>Their</u> attempts are almost always comical, not <u>being able</u> to move supplies without <u>loosing</u> at least one package on the <u>route</u>. <u>No error.</u>

    A. Their

    B. being able

    C. loosing

    D. route

    E. No error

The answer is C.
The underlined word has one too many 'O's, and should be written as losing.

3.   At least two of the seven <u>defendents</u> <u>want</u> a delay, <u>saying</u> they need more time <u>to prepare</u> for trial. <u>No error.</u>

    A.   defendents

    B.   want

    C.   saying

    D.   to prepare

    E.   No eror

The answer is A.
The word listed is misspelled frequently, and is correctly spelled defendants.

4.   The surfer <u>was bit</u> by a shark, but <u>got</u> his revenge when he <u>caught</u> him and <u>ate</u> it for dinner. <u>No error</u>

    A.   was bit

    B.   got

    C.   caught

    D.   ate

    E.   No error

The answer is A.
as the appropriate past conjugation is was bitten.

5.   A portrait of a <u>women</u> <u>had been</u> painted onto an iceberg, which was precariously <u>perched</u> on the edge of a melting <u>piece</u> of glacier. <u>No error</u>

A.   women

B.   had been

C.   perched

D.   piece

E.   No error

The answer is A.
The underlined word should be singular, woman, as indicated by the verb tense as well as the lead-in "a" (plural would be the).

Read the following paragraph and answer the questions that follow.

There was a steaming mist in all the hollows, and it roamed in its forlornness up the hill, like an evil spirit, seeking rest and finding none. A clammy and intensely cold mist, it made its way through the air in ripples that visibly followed and overspread one another, as the waves of an unwholesome sea might do. It was dense enough to shut out everything from the light of the coach-lamps but these its own workings, and a few yards of road; and the reek of the laboring horses steamed into it, as if they had made it at all.

6. **The description of this scene gives the impression that it is:**

   A.   an oppressive journey.

   B.   an enlightening route.

   C.   a contemplative traveling discussion.

   D.   an entertaining troupe making way to the next show.

   E.   None of these things is true.

The answer is A.
Choice B is incorrect because there are no descriptive words that indicate "enlightening". C is incorrect as there is no discussion, and D is also incorrect in that there is no reference whatsoever to justify this is true.

7. **What is the main idea of this passage?**

   A.   Weather sets the stage in any narrative.

   B.   The coach horses were not up to the task of the road.

   C.   It was a dark and cold night, relatively unsuitable for travel.

   D.   One of the coach-lamps was unlit, making it difficult to see.

   E.   An English countryside scene is perfect for a scary setting.

The answer is C.
While all options may be true, the only one that is correct on a high level without excluding other pieces of the narrative makes C the best answer.

8.   The author's purpose is to:

   A.   Inform

   B.   Entertain

   C.   Persuade

   D.   Narrate

   E.   Analyze

The answer is D.
The author is simply narrating the setting for the action of the plot.

Read the following passage and answer the questions that follow.

Everyone called him Pop Eye. Even in those days when I was a skinny thirteen-year-old I thought he probably knew about his nickname but didn't care. His eyes were too interested in what lay up ahead to notice us barefoot kids.

He looked like someone who had seen or known great suffering and hadn't been able to forget it. His large eyes in his large head stuck out further than anyone else's - like they wanted to lave the surface of his face. They made you think of someone who can't get out the house quickly enough.

Pop Eye wore the same white linen suit every day. His trousers snagged onto hi sony knees in the sloppy heat. Some days he wore a clown's nose. His nose was already big. he didn't need that red light bulb. But for reasons we couldn't think of he wore the red nose on certain days that may have meant something to him. We never saw him smile. And on those days he wore the clowns nose you found yourself looking away because you never saw such sadness.

237

9.   What is the main idea of the passage?

   A.   The main character was a generally sad man, disinterested in the scene around him.

   B.   The main character cannot remember the thirteen-year-old kid.

   C.   The physical appearance of the main character was awkward.

   D.   The main character was so poor that he only had one suit.

   E.   None of these represent the main idea of the passage.

The answer is A.
While options B through D are correct according to the passage, the overall idea is encompassed in A.

10.   From the passage, one can infer that:

   A.   Pop Eye is surrounded by family.

   B.   Pop Eye works as a clown.

   C.   The narrator is related to Pop Eye.

   D.   Pop Eye lives a lonely life.

   E.   The narrator has done well for himself.

The answer is D.
No other options are supported by information in the passage.

11.   **What is the author's purpose in writing this passage?**

    A.   To entertain

    B.   To narrate

    C.   To describe

    D.   To persuade

    E.   To make demands

The answer is C.
The author does describe the scene more than any other options. The author sets the scene for future plot development.

12.   **The author implies that :**

    A.   the main character had secret talents.

    B.   the main character had great sadness.

    C.   the narrator was related to the main character.

    D.   the main character was generally neat and tidy.

    E.   the narrator was homeless.

The answer is B.
This fact is directly stated in the last paragraph.

Read the following passage excerpted from Biography.com and choose the best answer to the questions that follow.

A prolific artist, Austrian composer Wolfgang Mozart created a string of operas, concertos, symphonies and sonatas that profoundly shaped classical music. Over the years, Mozart aligned himself with a variety of European venues and patrons, composing hundreds of works that included sonatas, symphonies, masses, concertos and operas, marked by vivid emotion and sophisticated textures.

During the time when he worked for Archbishop Hieronymus von Colleredo, young Mozart had the opportunity to work in several different musical genres composing symphonies, string quartets, sonatas and serenades and a few operas. He developed a passion for violin concertos producing what came to be the only five he wrote.   In 1776, he turned his efforts toward piano concertos, culminating in the Piano Concerto Number 9 in E flat major in early 1777. In Salzburg in 1779, Wolfgang Amadeus Mozart produced a series of church works, including the Coronation Mass. He also composed another opera for Munich, Ideomeneo in 1781.

13.   Who is the target audience of this passage?

   A. Artists.

   B. Austrians.

   C. Catholics.

   D. A person interested in classical music.

   E. None of these are accurate.

The answer is D.
While the other options use listed words in the selection, the answer most correct is D.

14. **What is the main idea of the previous passage?**

   A. Mozart had a sister that also performed with him.

   B. Mozart's father was his promoter.

   C. The Catholic church was supportive of Mozart's talent.

   D. Many operas and other pieces were composed by Mozart before he was 25 years old.

   E. The rapid development and appreciation of Mozart's music.

The answer is E.
While all of the items are facts and listed in the context of the passage, the overall main idea is expressed in E.

15. **What is the author's purpose in writing this?**

   A. To describe

   B. To narrate

   C. To entertain

   D. To inform

   E. To argue

The answer is D.
The author is providing the reader with information about musicality and progress of Mozart's development.

16. **From reading this passage, we can conclude that:**

    A.   Mozart wrote several complex pieces of music at a young age.

    B.   There were not many composers as young and talented as Mozart.

    C.   There was a special relationship between the Catholic church and Mozart's family.

    D.   There were not as many composers in Austria as other countries.

    E.   None of these are accurate.

The answer is A.
Options B through D express opinions not supported in the passage.

17. **Which of the following is not a musical genre?**

    A.   Opera

    B.   Sonnet

    C.   Symphony

    D.   Concerto

    E.   Quartet

The answer is B.
A Sonnet is a poem form while a Sonota is a musical form. This correct form is directly listed in the passage.

Read the following paragraph and answer the questions that follow.

(1)Outside, the late afternoon sun slanted down in the yard, throwing into gleaming brightness the dogwood trees that were solid masses of white blossoms against the background of new green. (2)The twins' horses were hitched in the driveway, big animals, red as their masters' hair; and around the horses' legs quarreled the pack of lean, nervous possum hounds that accompanied Stuart and Brent wherever they went. (3)A little aloof, as became and aristocrat, lay a black-spotted carriage dog, puzzle on paws, patiently waiting for the boys to go home to supper.

18. **What is the main idea of this passage?**

    A.   The passage is describing an afternoon outdoor setting.

    B.   The twins had very poised animals.

    C.   Certain concessions should be made for dogs.

    D.   The difficulties of travel in thick blossoming forests.

    E.   None of these covey the main idea of the passage.

The answer is A.
Option B is not true, as the dogs were quarreling around the horses' legs; Option C is not conveyed in the passage; Option D is not relayed int he passage anywhere about the group traveling.

19. **What is the author's main purpose?**

    A.   To inform

    B.   To entertain

    C.   To describe

    D.   To narrate

    E.   To record

The answer is C.
The author is simply describing the scene.

20.   What type of sentence is the second sentence?

  A. Simple

  B. Compound

  C. Complex

  D. Complex-Compound

  E. Dependent clause

The answer is D.
A semi-colon is even used, which is typical to conjoin to complex sentences. With the use of conjunctions (and), this also makes it compound.

Read the following paragraph from Wikipedia and answer the question that follows.

Isaac Newton built the first practical reflecting telescope and developed a theory of colour based on the observation that a prism decomposes white light into the many colors of the visible spectrum. He formulated an empirical law of cooling, studied the speed of sound, and introduced the notion of a Newtonian fluid. In addition to his work on calculus, as a mathematician Newton contributed to the study of power series, generalized the binomial theorem to non-integer exponents, developed a method for approximating the roots of a function, and classified most of the cubic plane curves.

21.   **What is the main idea of this passage?**

    A.   Power series is an important part of scientific discovery.

    B.   Fluid engineering is about the empirical law of cooling.

    C.   Through telescopes, scientists have made discoveries that have helped many people.

    D.   Newton was a mathematician and a scientist.

    E.   None of the above.

The answer is D.
While the first three options are correct, the fourth gives a higher-level viewpoint of the overall passage.

Read the following paragraph from *Popular Mechanics* and answer the question that follows.

We've been finding planets beyond our solar system for two decades now, but there are good reasons why it's taken so long to find the first forming world. For one thing, Stephanie Sallum says, planets spend only a brief period of their long lives in formation. Simply looking at the the odds, "it's unlikely that you'll come across a planet when it's still forming," she says.

22.   **The author's purpose is to**

    A.   Describe

    B.   Inform

    C.   Persuade

    D.   Narrate

    E.   Summarize

The answer is B.
Option B is correct in that the discussion is about the new discovery of plants and the reasons that it has been hard to discover.

Read the following paragraph from National Geographic and answer the question.

So far, more than 150 countries – from Sudan to Suriname and from Kiribati to Kyrgyzstan – have outlined for United Nations negotiators just how, when, and by how much each would cut carbon dioxide over the next several decades. If an agreement is reached, it would mark the first serious global commitment to reduce the pollution that is warming the planet, souring the oceans, and causing seas to rise.

23.   What type of organizational pattern is the author using?

    A.   Comparison and Contrast

    B.   Generalization

    C.   Cause and Effect

    D.   Simple Listing

    E.   Analogy

The answer is C.
The author lists some causes and effects for fighting global warming.
Read the following paragraph from *Antiques and Fine Art* and answer the following question.

Since the colonial period, the Atlantic Ocean has operated both as a barrier between America and Europe and as a conduit for international exchanges of peoples, goods, and ideas. It spurred commerce and enterprise that was the basis for both national economic activity and personal fortune. The activities in America's great harbors and port cities also supported the nation's cultural development, prompting the rise of schools of maritime and landscape painting, as well as portraiture.

24.   Which organizational pattern does the author use?

    A.   Comparison and Contrast

    B.   Simple Listing

    C.   Cause and Effect

    D.   Definition

    E.   Description

The answer is A.
Since the author is demonstrating differences between America and Europe around the Atlantic Ocean, the correct answer is (A).

Read the following quote and answer the following question.

"I don't think about whether people will remember me or not. I've been an okay person. I've learned a lot. I've taught people a thing or two. That's what's important." – Julia Child

25.   The quote primarily:

    A.   describes.

    B.   informs.

    C.   entertains.

    D.   narrates.

    E.   lists.

The answer is B.
Since the quote telling us how Julia Child saw her life, the correct answer here is (B).

26.   Addressing someone absent or something inhuman as though present and able to respond describes a figure of speech known as:

A.   personification

B.   synecdoche

C.   metonymy

D.   apostrophe

E.   rhetorical strategy

The answer is A.
Personification is taking something inhuman and giving it personal traits (such as responding).

Read the following paragraphs and answer the questions that follows.

I.   At the end of the period, the artistic temperament of the painter undergoes a profound modification; it reflects a set of assimilated romantic ideas, expands the grandeur of classical art, and, while in the early works the love for the antique style throughout the popular subjects with inanimate edifice with the classic treatment as well as characterless, mythological subjects in the frescoes. The painter's figures assume heroic proportions, exude solemn expressions, and everything seems to come alive in a life more lush, more monumental and simple at the same time...

II.   Overall, we find an artist's determined personality, animated by a continuous and rapid progress, the result of a clear conscience and scrupulous study fiery aspects of reality with which can be sympathized, of an intense search of technical development, the assimilation of many and beautiful expressions of art. So he states, from the beginning of his artistic activity, a teacher of exceptional importance, which rises with noble means and personal and solid, without resorting to defiant rage, the glitz, the stylism that characterize so remarkable part of the art of his time.

III. Serra, Luigi. Domenico Zampieri detto Il Domenichino. Rome: Casa Editrice del Bollettino d'Arte, Del Ministero Della P. Istruzione. 1909. pp11-12.

27.   Where does the excerpt originate?

    A.   Webster's Dictionary

    B.   Luigi Serra

    C.   Domenico Zampieri

    D.   World Book Encyclopedia

    E.   Wikipedia

The answer is B.
It is listed as the source directly below the passage, and in the format, Serra is the author. Zampieri is the subject of the material.

28.   In the second paragraph, the second sentence can best be described as:

    A.   compound.

    B.   complex.

    C.   run-on.

    D.   a fragment.

    E.   compound-complex.

The answer is C.
which is just a fact that you need to know when answering questions in this section.

29.   This, H. (2006). Food for Tomorrow? How the Scientific Discipline of Molecular Gastronomy Could Change the Way We Eat. *EMBO Reports*, 7(11), 1062-1066.

In the citation, 1062 provides what information?

A.   Date printed

B.   Date accessed

C.   First page of reference

D.   Last page of reference

E.   None of these are correct

The answer is C.
The first page of the reference cited.

30.   **In the citation above, the (11) refers to:**

A.   the eleventh article in the magazine.

B.   the eleventh article published by this author.

C.   there are eleven articles on gastronomy in this issue.

D.   there are eleven authors.

E.   this is the eleventh issue in the series, in volume seven.

The answer is E.
The citation for the correct issue in the correctly listed volume.

31.   In the *EMBO* citation above, 7 refers to what?

    A.   The number of volumes this has magazine has published in 2006

    B.   How many articles have discussed gastronomy in the magazine's history

    C.   The seventh report for this issue

    D.   Pagination

    E.   Tagnemics

The answer is A.
as it lists the correct volume from the original citation.

32.   **Bernstein, M. (2002). 10 tips on writing the living Web.** *A List Apart: For People Who Make Websites, 149.* **Retrieved from http://www.alistapart.com/articles/writeliving is a citation example of a:**

    A.   newspaper.

    B.   book.

    C.   online periodical.

    D.   abstract.

    E.   none of these selections are accurate.

The answer is C.
Option C is correct, which should be evident not only by the title but also the website listed in the citation.

33. 2. Weinstein, "Plato's *Republic*," 452–53.
This is an example of:

A. note style.

B. duplicate style.

C. bibliography.

D. APA style.

E. MLA style.

The answer is B.
as if it was any of the others, it would have a complete first and last name as well as place of publication and year.

34. Kossinets, Gueorgi, and Duncan J. Watts. "Origins of Homophily in an Evolving Social Network." *American Journal of Sociology* 115 (2009): 405–50. Accessed February 28, 2010. doi:10.1086/599247.

Which style is this?

A. MLA

B. APA

C. Chicago

D. New York

E. None of these

The answer is C.
The year comes later in Chicago format and the second name is listed in first name last name order.

35.   Maxmen, Amy. "How Ebola Found Fertile Ground in Sierra Leone's Chaotic Capital." National Geographic. 27 January, 2015. Web. 16 November, 2015.

This is an example of what kind of citation format?

A.   MLA

B.   APA

C.   Chicago

D.   Turabian

E.   None of these

The answer is A.
as this is MLA citation format. These are facts, the differences between citation types that should be known for the test.

36.   In the citation above, what does 27 January 2015 reference?

A.   Reference date

B.   Publication date

C.   Editing date

D.   Web upload date

E.   None of these

The answer is B.
as this is is the publication date. The reference date comes at the end. Any editing or version dates would come after the title with an editor's name.

37.   Treverton, Gregory F. "The Changed Target." *Intelligence for an Age of Terror.* Cambridge: Cambridge UP, 2009. 24-25. Print. What does print reference?

A.   Magazine article

B.   Newspaper article

C.   Printed web source

D.   Book

E.   None of these

The answer is D.
The "print" gives that fact.

Read the following paragraph from the *National Independent Schools Magazine* and answer the questions that follow.

The bias against introverted students is embedded in our educational system: years of unrelenting focus on cooperative learning, thinking aloud, and talking-as-learning, with grades for class participation, required public speaking (often now as a disproportionate pedagogical focus displacing more traditional forms of scholarship and substantive mastery), and a pervasive, almost normative, value placed on being social and well liked, particularly in a large-group context. In sum, the classroom focus is now too often on "doing," in sacrifice to "thinking."

38. **What is meant by the word "un- relenting" in the first sentence?**

    A. Continuing

    B. Protective

    C. Pervasive

    D. Cautious

    E. Reckless

The answer is A.
You should be able to be determined through careful reading of the passage. This is a key to succeeding in this section, being able to analyze and replace words with similar meanings.

39. **What is the author's tone?**

    A. Aseptic

    B. Analytical

    C. Disbelieving

    D. Disapproving

    E. Scornful

The answer is D.
The author uses words that show disapproval of bias against introverted students throughout the passage.

40.   What type of organizational pattern is the author using?

    A.   Classification

    B.   Explanation

    C.   Comparison and Contrast

    D.   Cause and Effect

    E.   Entertaining

The answer is D.
The author mentions the things that are being pushed onto children that may not learn best in that style and has clearly stated "bias against" - this would be most correctly listed as effect and cause, but is the best option as it is not typical to list "effect and cause" in choices.

41.   Who would be the intended audience of this excerpt?

    A.   Politicians, for funding purposes.

    B.   Social workers, for counseling purposes.

    C.   Teachers, for refocusing efforts.

    D.   Parents, for normative adjustments.

    E.   None of these are applicable.

The answer is C.
There is no mention of funding or politics; there is no mention of social workers or counseling; there is no mention of parents or adjustments. Though any of these groups and purposes may be targeted, we can only answer questions based on the information presented in the selections within the test. Be sure to not bring outside information into answering questions.

Read the following passage from Roll of Thunder, Hear My Cry and answer the questions that follow.

My youngest brother paid no attention to me. Grasping more firmly his newspaper-wrapped notebook and his tin-can lunch of cornbread and oil sausages, he continued to concentrate on the dusty road. He lagged several feet behind my other brothers, Stacey and Christopher-John, and me, attempting to keep the rusty Mississippi dust from swelling with each step and drifting back upon his shiny black shoes and the cuffs of his corduroy pants by lifting each foot high before setting it gently down again. Always meticulously neat, six-year-old Little Man never allowed dirt or tears or stains to mar anything he owned. Today was no exception.

"You keep it up and make us late for school, Mama's gonna wear you out," I threatened, pulling with exasperation at the high collar of the Sunday dress Mama had made me wear for the first day of school - as if that event were something special. It seemed to me that showing up at school all on a bright August-like October morning made for running the cool forest trails and wading barefoot in the forest pond was concession enough; Sunday clothing was asking too much. Christopher-John and Stacey were not too pleased about the clothing or school either. Only Little Man, just beginning his school career, found the prospects of both intriguing.

42. What is the meaning of the word "meticulously" in the next to last sentence in the first paragraph?

   A. Many

   B. Very

   C. Exceptionally

   D. Rarely

   E. Fairly

The answer is C.
While B and E may be correct, it is not emphatic enough and the other options are not applicable or opposite.

43. **What is the overall organizational pattern used in this passage?**

    A. Generalization

    B. Cause and Effect

    C. Addition

    D. Descriptive

    E. Informational

The answer is D.
The author describes the scene of the children walking down the dirt road.

44. **What is the author's tone?**

    A. Disbelieving

    B. Exasperated

    C. Informative

    D. Optimistic

    E. None of these are correct.

The answer is B.
The sister is the narrator for this passage and she actually uses the word "exasperation" in the first sentence of the second paragraph.

Read the following passage from Pride and Prejudice and answer the questions that follow.

Mr. Bennet was so odd a mixture of quick parts, sarcastic humour, reserve, and caprice, that the experience of three-and-twenty years had been insufficient to make his wife understand his character. Her mind was less difficult to develop. She was a woman of mean understanding, little information, and uncertain temper. When she was discontented, she fancied herself nervous. The business of her life was to get her daughters married; its solace was visiting and news.

Mr. Bennet was among the earliest of those who waited on Mr. Bingley. He had always intended to visit him, though to the last always assuring his wife that he should not go; and till the evening after the visit was paid she had no knowledge of it. It was then disclosed in the following manner. Observing his second daughter employed in trimming a hat, he suddenly addressed her with:

"I hope Mr. Bingley will like it, Lizzy."

45.   What is the overall organizational pattern of this passage?

    A. Generalization

    B. Cause and Effect

    C. Addition

    D. Summary

    E. Informational

The answer is A.
Because it was a description of the generalities with both Mr. as well as Mrs. Bennet. There is no cause and effect described, and C as well as D are not correct. E may be a tempting choice, but it is not relaying information - when data and facts (such as science) are given, that is when it's appropriate to select informational.

46.   What is the meaning of the phrase "uncertain temper" in the third
       sentence?

    A. Hot tempered

    B. Quixotic emotions

    C. Unusually morose

    D. Generally happy

    E. None of these apply

The answer is B.
Answer A may seem a likely choice, except temper is not being used literally
in this passage. C and D give one extreme or another, and that is not what is
implied in the context of the passage either.

47.   What is the organizational pattern of the second paragraph?

    A. Cause and Effect

    B. Classification

    C. Addition

    D. Explanation

    E. None of these things

The answer is D.
By selecting D, the explanation is how the second paragraph is organized, the
reader shows that he or she understood that the narrator is providing
explanation as to why Mr. Bennet didn't previously tell his wife about
visiting Mr. Bingley and then why he did.

Read the following passage from Wuthering Heights and answer the questions that follow.

Before passing the threshold, I pause to admire a quantity of grotesque carving lavished over the front, and especially about the principal door; above which, among a wilderness of crumbling griffins and shameless little boys, I detected the date '1500,' and the name 'Hareton Earnshaw.' I would have made a few comments, and requested a short history of the plane from the surly owner; but his attitude at the door appeared to demand my speedy entrance, or complete departure, and I had no desire to aggregate his impatience previous to inspecting the penetralium.

48.   What is the author's overall organizational pattern?

   A. Classification

   B. Cause and Effect

   C. Definition

   D. Comparison and Contrast

   E. None of these things

The answer is E.
The offered answers for organizational pattern of the passage are not correct; therefore, answer E is correct.

49.   The author's tone in the passage is one of:

    A. Inquisition

    B. Excitement

    C. Surliness

    D. Concern

    E. Impatience

The answer is A.
The speaker actually says a few comments would have been made about what is seen in the room. Answer B is not conveyed in the passage. C, D, and E are words used to describe the male's attitude in the passage, so they could be immediately eliminated.

50.   The most similar way to rephrase "I had no desire to aggregate his impatience" in context of the passage would be:

    A. I wanted to keep him happy

    B. I didn't want to make him mad

    C. I didn't want to stay around

    D. I wanted him to quickly inspect the penetralium

    E. None of these are approximations

The answer is B.
The correct rephrasing is B for most accurately representing a rephrased sentence. While A may be true from analysis, it is not correct syntax to match the phrase pulled _from_ the passage. C and D are just not correct choices (D actually skips part of the sentence and tricks a reader moving too quickly by using the ending of the actual paragraph - make sure you read carefully!)

Description of the Examination

The Spanish Language examination is designed to measure knowledge and ability equivalent to that of students who have completed two to four semesters of college Spanish language study. The exam focuses on skills typically achieved from the end of the first year through the second year of college study; material taught during both years is incorporated into a single exam.

The examination contains approximately 120 questions to be answered in approximately 90 minutes. Some of these are pretest questions that will not be scored. There are three separately timed sections. The three sections are weighted so that each question contributes equally to the total score. Any time candidates spend on tutorials or providing personal information is in addition to the actual testing time.

There are two Listening sections and one Reading section. Each section has its own timing requirements.

- The two Listening sections together are approximately 30 minutes in length. The amount of time candidates have to answer a question varies according to the section and does not include the time they spend listening to the test material.
- The Reading section is 60 minutes in length.

Most colleges that award credit for the Spanish Language exam award either two or four semesters of credit, depending on the candidate's test scores.

Knowledge and Skills Required
Questions on the Spanish Language examination require candidates to comprehend written and spoken Spanish. The subject matter is drawn from the following abilities. The percentages next to the main topics indicate the approximate percentage of exam questions on that ability.

60%   **Section III: Reading**
- 16% Part A: Discrete sentences (vocabulary and structure)
- 20% Part B: Short cloze passages (vocabulary and structure)
- 24% Part C: Reading passages and authentic stimulus materials (reading comprehension)

15%   **Section I:**
- Listening: Rejoinders
- Listening comprehension

through short oral
exchanges

25%   **Section II:**
- Listening: Dialogues
  and Narratives
- Listening
  comprehension
  through longer spoken
  selections

SECTION I

Listening: Rejoinders

Directions: You will hear short conversations or parts of conversations. You will then hear four responses, designated (A), (B), (C), and (D). After you hear the four responses, select the response that most logically continues or completes the conversation. Fill in the corresponding oval on your answer sheet. Neither the answer choices nor the conversations will be printed in your test booklet, so you must listen very carefully. You will have 10 seconds to choose your response before the next conversation begins.

Número 1.   **MALE**   Tuve una incidencia en mi computador de mi puesto de trabajo.

            FEMALE
- A.   El técnico llegará rápido.
- B.   El técnico no fue a la cita.
- C.   El técnico acudirá a su cita.
- D.   El técnico llegará rápidamente.

Número 2.   **MALE**   ¿Por qué los niños no fueron a comer?

            FEMALE
- A.   Porque los niños están comiendo pollo.
- B.   Porque ellos comen papás fritas.
- C.   Porque están enfermos de tanto comer.
- D.   Porque estuvieron jugando con sus amigos.

Número 3.   **FEMALE**   ¿Has quedado agotado después de caminar?

            MALE
- A.   Me gusta este ejercicio.
- B.   Siempre lo hago.
- C.   He tenido dolencias en el tobillo y la rodilla.
- D.   Al contrario, estoy más animado para volverlo a hacer.

Número 4.   **FEMALE**   Cambiaré de trabajo el próximo verano.

            MALE
- A.   ¿Te incrementarán el sueldo en tu actual compañía?
- B.   ¿Recibirás el ascenso en pocos días?
- C.   ¿Te pagarán más dinero?
- D.   Serás un desempleado más.

Número 5.   MALE   Como llegó a la Avenida 7ª con calle 13.
FEMALE
A. Debes preguntar primero a un vecino.
B. ¿Eres un extranjero?
C. Debes cruzar el puente y luego girar hacia la derecha.
D. Tardarás un poco en llegar porque es bastante lejos.

Número 6.   MALE   No puedo llegar tarde a casa.
FEMALE
A. Si apenas comienza la reunión.
B. ¿No tienes dinero?
C. ¿Cuál es tu nacionalidad?
D. ¿Cuál es tu comida favorita?

Número 7.   MALE   ¿Harás mucho dinero con tu compañía?
FEMALE
A. No, porque viajé a Chile.
B. Sí, porque tengo muchos clientes.
C. Sí, porque me casé.
D. No, porqué trabajé en 1980.

Número 8.   MALE   Hace muchos días no veo a mi familia.
FEMALE
A. ¿Tienes familia?
B. ¿Tu familia vive lejos?
C. ¿Viviste en Brasil?
D. ¿Qué te gusta ver en cine?

Número 9.   MALE   ¿Cómo estuvo el concierto de Rock?
FEMALE
A. Fui con mis amigos.
B. Va a estar genial.
C. Fue una experiencia inolvidable.
D. Será muy bueno.

Número 10.   MALE   ¿Me vas a acompañar a la fiesta?
FEMALE
A. Si, estuvo muy interesante.
B. No, fue muy aburrida.
C. Seguramente.
D. Verdad! ¿Cuándo fue?

Número 11.   MALE   ¿Irás al centro comercial?
FEMALE
A. Mi hermana te mandó saludes.
B. Si me invitas a comer.
C. Ayer, fui al estadio.
D. ¿Tú me entregaste lo que necesito?

Número 12. **FEMALE** ¿Para qué ahorras tanto dinero en tu alcancía?.

  MALE A. Para irme de vacaciones con mi familia.

  B. Me fui de vacaciones con mi familia.

  C. Fui a Paris.

  D. Estuve con mi familia en Disney Word.

Número 13. **FEMALE** ¿Por qué hablaste tanto de Europa?

  MALE A. Estuve en un tour.

  B. No tuve dinero.

  C. Mi familia vive en Ecuador.

  D. Soy Panameño.

Número 14. **FEMALE** ¿Te vas a ir en carro?

  MALE A. El autobús es rojo.

  B. Si llueve.

  C. La semana pasada llovió.

  D. Voy con mi mamá.

Número 15. **FEMALE** Seré la mejor de la clase.

  MALE A. Si te dedicas a estudiar todos los días.

  B. Si no fueras inteligente.

  C. Si mantuvieras en desorden tus horarios de estudio.

  D. Si eres perezoso.

Número 16. **FEMALE** ¿Qué sucede si Pablo no puede venir a acompañarte?

  MALE A. Fui a la estación de tren.

  B. Me iría con mi primo.

  C. Trabajé todo el día.

  D. Mi perro me acompañó al parque.

Número 17. **FEMALE** ¿Cuándo fue la última vez que visitaste Cartagena?

  MALE A. Fue una experiencia inolvidable.

  B. El verano pasado.

  C. Fui con mi hermana.

  D. Cartagena es Fantástico.

Número 18. **FEMALE** Podemos hacer la comida en nuestra casa.

 MALE A. Fui a una barbacoa la semana pasada.

 B. A menos que sea sin mis amigos.

 C. cuando entregues el domicilio.

 D. Siempre y cuando todos ayuden después a limpiarla.

SECTION II

Listening: Dialogues and Narratives

Directions: You will hear a series of dialogues, news reports, narratives, and announcements. Listen carefully, as each selection will only be spoken once. One or more questions with four possible answers are printed in your test booklet. They will not be spoken. After each selection has been read, choose the best answer choice for each question and fill in the corresponding oval on your answer sheet. You will be given 12 seconds to answer each question.

Selección número 1

En el banco

JUAN: Buenas noches.

MARIO: Buenas noches. ¿Qué necesita?

JUAN: He venido a cambiar este cheque bancario de cinco mil dólares.

MARIO: ¿Me permites tu número de identificación?

JUAN: Hm-m, lo siento. Tengo mi tarjeta, pero soy menor de edad. Aún no tengo un número de identificación.

MARIO: Pero de esta manera no puedo entregarte el dinero en efectivo.

JUAN: Debes hablar directamente con el director del banco para que te colabore con este tema. Pero por el momento él no se encuentra. Debes esperarlo--por lo menos media hora.

MARIO: ¿Estás seguro que él me puede hacer el favor?

JUAN: Sí, porque muchas personas han podido, gracias al permiso de las empresas donde laboran.

MARIO: Perfecto. Entonces lo esperaré.

NARRADOR: Ahora contesta las preguntas 19, 20, y 21

19. **¿Cuál fue el motivo por el cual Juan visitó el banco?**

    A. Fue a modificar su número de identificación porque estaba incorrecto.

    B. Fue a reclamar un dinero que le consignaron.

    C. Fue a cambiar un cheque.

    D. Fue a hablar con el director del banco porque estaba confundido.

20. ¿Por qué le negaron el cambio del cheque bancario a Juan?

   A. Porque el valor del cheque superaba los cinco mil dólares.

   B. Porque Juan era menor de edad y la ley lo prohibía.

   C. Porque el cheque no tenía fecha.

   D. Porque Juan no presentó su número de identificación.

21. ¿Qué tuvo que hacer Juan para que le cambiarán el cheque bancario?

   A. Tuvo que hacer unas llamadas a la sucursal principal.

   B. Tuvo que hablar con el director del banco.

   C. Tuvo que pedir unas autorizaciones por parte de la empresa donde trabajaba.

   D. Tuvo que esperar al gerente de la empresa donde él trabajaba por media hora, para que le autorizara su cheque.

En la biblioteca

ALEXA: Buenas tardes.

SERGIO: Buenas tardes. Vine a hacer un préstamo de un libro.

ALEXA: Claro que sí, pero dime, ¿cuál es el libro?

SERGIO: Se llama fundamentos de la economía de Edmund Burke. ¿Me ayudas a encontrarlo?

ALEXA: Si, este libro se encuentra en la sección II de Economía.

SERGIO: ¿Por cuánto tiempo me puedes prestar este libro?,

ALEXA: Sólo te lo puedes llevar por quince días y recuerda que si superas ese tiempo y no las has entregado, la biblioteca te cobrará una multa y no podrás volver a pedir libros prestados hasta nueva orden. Debes estar consciente de eso.

SERGIO: ¿Y de cuánto es la multa?

ALEXA: La multa es de cinco dólares.

SERGIO: Listo. Muchas gracias por tu ayuda.

NARRADOR: Ahora contesta las preguntas de 22, 23, y 24.

22. **¿Qué estaba haciendo Sergio en la biblioteca?**

    A. Estaba leyendo el libro, «Fundamentos de Economía».

    B. Estaba estudiando para una prueba de economía.

    C. Estaba leyendo la biografía de Edmund Burke.

    D. Prestó un libro de Edmund Burke.

23. **¿Cuánto tiempo le prestarán el libro a Sergio?**

    A. Dos semanas.

    B. Una semana.

    C. Mes y medio.

    D. Cincuenta días.

24. **¿Qué sucede si Sergio no entrega el libro a la biblioteca en el tiempo estipulado?**

    A. La biblioteca le privará los servicios a Sergio.

    B. Le cobrarán el libro como nuevo.

    C. Lo reportan con la biblioteca.

    D. Debe asistir a unas conferencias de capacitación y concientización

Selección número 3

En el zoológico

EDWIN: Buenos días Martha, el día de hoy te enseñaré el animal más hermoso de este zoológico.

MARTHA: Que bueno, estaré atenta a tu información y también a tus recomendaciones.

EDWIN: El animal que te mostraré es el búfalo.

MARTHA: ¡Fabuloso! Pero dime, ¿Es peligroso este animal?

EDWIN: No. Pero cuando se encuentra en momentos de peligro embiste con furiosos bramidos. Por ejemplo en este caso, lo está haciendo porque nos acaba de ver.

MARTHA: ¡Guau!

EDWIN: También te quiero contar que el búfalo es oriundo de Asia y siempre tiene una única cría.

MARTHA: Gracias, Edwin.

EDWIN: Con gusto. Recuerda registrar tu nombre en la entrada del zoológico para tomar tu asistencia.

NARRADOR: Ahora contesta las preguntas 25, 26, y 27.

25. **¿Qué harán Edwin y Martha en el zoológico?**

    A. Harán un recorrido por todo el zoológico.

    B. Conocerán a un animal en específico.

    C. Participarán de una muestra de animales salvajes.

    D. Atenderán una serie de recomendaciones por parte del zoológico.

26. **Según lo que le planteó Edwin a Martha, el animal que narran ¿es furioso?**

    A. Sí, porque embiste sin alguna discriminación.

    B. No, pero si se altera en momentos de peligro.

    C. Sí, porque cuando ve personas, se altera demasiado.

    D. No, porque por naturaleza del búfalo es furioso.

27. **¿Qué tuvo que hacer Martha cuando se fue del zoológico?**

    A. Pagar su estadía en el zoológico.

    B. Confirmar su asistencia para la próxima visita.

    C. Consignar su nombre en la recepción del zoológico.

    D. Registrar la huella en el lector

Selección número 4

En una planta de producción

LAURA: Quiero que me informes sobre la producción del día de hoy.

ERIKA: Claro. Pero antes quisiera decirte que se dañaron dos máquinas selladoras y eso afectó la producción.

LAURA: Hm-m. Entonces reportaré esta novedad al departamento de mantenimiento. De todas maneras cuéntame, ¿cuántas pacas empacaron?

ERIKA: Sí. Se empacaron doscientas pacas de bombones, cien pacas de chicle y trescientas pacas de mentas.

LAURA: Sí estuvo bastante regular. Me preocupa porque estoy recibiendo muchas quejas por parte del cliente y una de ellas es precisamente que no estamos entregando los pedidos a tiempo.

ERIKA: De esta manera los indicadores bajan y nos perjudicamos todos los empleados.

NARRADOR: Ahora contesta las preguntas 28, 29, y 30.

28. **¿Qué le pidió Laura a Erika?**

   A. Dos máquinas selladoras para cerrar unas pacas.

   B. Un informe para el departamento de mantenimiento.

   C. Los reportes de producción sobre las pacas empacadas.

   D. La producción de los últimos días.

29. **Al final de cuentas, ¿cuántas pacas se empacaron en total?**

   A. Trescientas pacas de bombón, cien de chicle y doscientas de menta.

   B. Cien de menta, doscientas de bombón y trescientas de chicle.

   C. Doscientas de chicle, trescientas de menta y cien de bombón.

   D. Seiscientas pacas de todos los productos.

30. **¿Últimamente por qué está recibiendo Laura quejas de los clientes?**

   A. Porque no están cumpliendo con el número de pedidos.

   B. Porque no están respetando los tiempos de entrega.

   C. Porque están entregando productos de mala calidad.

   D. Porque los productos están muy costosos.

En una clase de física

JORGE: El tiempo dispuesto para esta sesión de inquietudes es de una hora. Por lo tanto, las dudas del tema de «Termodinámica» para el examen, las resolveré rápidamente.

ALBERTO: Esta bien. He entendido muy bien el tema, pero tengo una duda muy importante.

JORGE: ¿Cuál es tu duda?

ALBERTO: Como tú nos has explicado, la termodinámica tiene como objetivo que conocer en qué condiciones se puede producir una reacción.

JORGE: Sí. Pero debes ser más específico con tu pregunta porque el tiempo corre y las horas vuelan.

ALBERTO: ¿La termodinámica considera el tiempo como variable?

JORGE: Muy buena pregunta, Alberto. Tienes razón. El tiempo no es una variable que considera la termodinámica, pero ésta si es muy importante en la industria para determinar si un proceso químico es rentable o no.

NARRADOR: Ahora contesta las preguntas 31, 32, y 33.

31. **De acuerdo con la narración, el profesor :**

   A. Dictará la clase explicando todo el tema de la termodinámica.

   B. Aclarará las dudas relacionadas con el tema.

   C. Entregará los exámenes de la termodinámica y resolverá las dudas del mismo.

   D. Preparará el examen de la termodinámica.

32. ¿A qué hace referencia la expresión, «el tiempo corre y las horas vuelan»?

A. La clase es muy corta y el profesor debe responder rápidamente a las dudas.

B. Las dudas deben preguntarlas rápidamente porque el profesor tiene mucho afán.

C. Las dudas deben ser muy concisas porque el profesor cuenta con poco tiempo.

D. El tiempo pasa rápidamente y el profesor sólo cuenta con una hora para responder a las dudas.

33. ¿En qué campo es importante la variable, «tiempo»?

A. En la industria, porque gracias a él, se establece si un proceso químico es viable o no.

B. En las investigaciones científicas, ya que con esta variable se sabe cuánto dura una reacción.

C. En los laboratorios, porque con el tiempo se analiza la caducidad de una reacción.

D. En ventas, ya que con esta variable se determinan si éstas son rentables o no.

Selección número 6

El origen del mundo

Muchos epílogos de nuestra historia aún son confusos e incluso desconocidos. Existen teorías apoyadas en realidades y testimonios. Pero todavía no convencen a las personas que se preguntan con insistencia acerca de eso. Continúan las controversias porque el mismo hombre modifica lo existente o lo oculta. En fin, la realidad sobre nuestros orígenes es muy compleja de descubrir, que lo único de que dependemos es de nuestro entorno, del medio ambiente, de lo divino para quien crea; o en su defecto, de las creencias que cada uno sigue en su vida cotidiana.

NARRADOR: Ahora contesta las preguntas 34, 35, y 36.

34. **Algunas partes de la historia del ser humano son:**

    A. Modificadas e inconclusas.

    B. Ambiguas y desconocidas.

    C. Imprecisas y confusas.

    D. Complejas y desconocidas.

35. **Las teorías que los científicos han expuesto a los seres humanos:**

    A. Son tan convincentes, que las personas creen plenamente en ellas.

    B. Generan dudas, ya que no están apoyados en testimonios reales.

    C. Están bien soportadas, pero aún no logran persuadir.

    D. No son verídicas porque no se han apoyado en testimonios reales.

36. **¿De qué depende el ser humano para sobrevivir?**

    A. De su entorno y del medio ambiente.

    B. De sus propios esfuerzos.

    C. Del dinero que gana por su trabajo.

    D. Del medio ambiente y de sí mismo.

Selección número 7

Programación neurolingüística

En el mundo entero existen muchas personas que sufren miles de enfermedades provenientes de sus mismas emociones que han terminado en finales caóticos. Día a día se logran muchos avances científicos que se llevan a cabo para mitigar todo ese tipo de enfermedades. Entre uno de ellas, se encuentra la denominada programación neurolingüística, gracias a unos científicos llamados Bandler y Grinder. Se desarrolló este sistema de aprendizaje que se utiliza como terapia, para ayudar a las personas que sufren de dolores. Ha sido tan efectivo que se han podido comprobar los efectos positivos que causan en una persona como por ejemplo: auto motivarse, perder los miedos, dejar hábitos malos y lo más asombroso--curar enfermedades. La programación neurolingüística es tan conocida que ya se ha difundido por diferentes partes del mundo para preparar a las personas que tengan responsabilidades importantes a su cargo.

NARRADOR: Ahora contesta las preguntas 37, 38, y 39.

37. ¿Cuál es el aspecto más grave que han provocado las enfermedades en las personas?

    A. Las alteraciones emocionales.

    B. Los descuidos en el cuidado de su salud.

    C. La falta de dinero para acudir al doctor.

    D. El sedentarismo.

38. ¿Por qué ha marcado la diferencia la programación neurolingüística en los últimos tiempos?

    A. Porque ha sido una de las terapias más innovadoras.

    B. Porque utiliza tecnología de punta para tratar a los pacientes.

    C. Porque le ha cambiado la vida a miles de personas debido a sus tratamientos.

    D. Porque sus creadores son científicos bastante creativos.

39. **La programación neurolingüística:**

    A. Ayuda en curar enfermedades pero no resuelve la auto-dependencia.

    B. Ayuda en mejorar los hábitos malos y a ser exitoso.

    C. Logra que una persona se auto-motive por sí misma.

    D. Logra que una persona pierda los miedos, pero no por un largo periodo.

Selección número 8
Del cigarrillo tradicional al cigarrillo electrónico

Los daños que provoca el cigarrillo en nuestro organismo son irreversibles, y en el mundo anualmente mueren seis millones de personas por causa de ese vicio. Esta es una de las amenazas grandes que vive entre la salud pública, ya que está afectando a los fumadores pasivos y a los niños. Actualmente, muchas personas han reemplazado el cigarrillo tradicional por el cigarrillo electrónico, queriendo atender las recomendaciones buenas que se han difundido por el mundo. Sin embargo este tema ha sido objeto de polémicas porque algunos señalan que los que fuman el cigarrillo electrónico tienen menos riesgos para la salud o nos ayuda en eliminar la dependencia con el cigarrillo tradicional. Por el otro lado, se afirma que este tipo de cigarrillo genera dependencia a la nicotina y problemas cardiovasculares--aun agravando más la situación.

NARRADOR: Ahora contesta las preguntas 40, 41, y 42.

40. **¿Cuántas personas mueren al año por causa del cigarrillo tradicional?**

    A. Seiscientos mil de personas.

    B. Seis millones de personas.

    C. Seis mil personas.

    D. Sesenta mil personas.

41. **¿Es buena para la salud el cigarrillo electrónico?**

    A. No, porque genera dependencia a la nicotina.

    B. No, porque genera problemas cardiovasculares.

    C. Sí, porque ayuda en eliminar la dependencia con la nicotina.

    D. Es ambiguo porque existen opiniones divididas.

42. **¿A qué invita la narración?**

    A. A que no fumen las personas porque sus consecuencias no son irreversibles.

    B. A informar sobre el riesgo del cigarrillo tradicional y del cigarrillo electrónico.

    C. A discutir sobre los usos del cigarrillo.

    D. A armar huelgas para que cierren las tabaqueras.

Selección número 9

La economía mundial

En los últimos años, la economía mundial ha logrado una transformación que ha conllevado el crecimiento de algunas economías y el declive de otras. Se ha visto marcada por cambios muy graves que se han traducido en problemas ambientales, desigualdades, y en problemas políticos, provocando conflictos internos y tensiones fuertes entre países. Esta problemática obliga a replantear los modelos económicos que son inestables, y que requieren una restructuración con miras a transformar la sociedad. También es muy importante que los altos mandos se comprometan a la realización de esos cambios porque si no existe ese compromiso, todo el esfuerzo para mejorar la economía mundial será en vano.

NARRADOR: Ahora contesta las preguntas 43, 44, y 45.

43. **¿Qué ha ocurrido con la economía de los países en los últimos años?**

    A. Algunos se han visto afectados fuertemente por la crisis económica mundial.

    B. Las economías tercermundistas han entrado en un proceso de expansión.

    C. Algunas economías han mejorado pero otras han entrado en crisis.

    D. Ha provocado muchas crisis internas.

44. **¿Qué ha afectado a la economía?**

    A. Los problemas políticos y las diferencias sociales.

    B. Los problemas ambientales y desigualdades.

    C. La burocracia.

    D. Los conflictos internos y externos de los países.

45. ¿Qué se debe hacer para que la economía se pueda mejorar?

A. Los gobiernos se deben comprometer a generar más empleo.

B. Se debe hacer una reestructuración del modelo económico.

C. Se deben generar oportunidades nuevas en el modelo social.

D. Ninguna de las anteriores.

Selección número 10

Nuestro ecosistema en peligro

El mundo cambia debido a las malas actuaciones del hombre. Nuestros ecosistemas han sido los más perjudicados por las decisiones que se han tomado, el uso que se les ha dado ha destruido a miles de especies y ha provocado que otras se encuentren en vía de extinción tal como el oso polar, el canguro, el tigre de bengala, los corales, la ballena, el pingüino, la tortuga de mar, el orangután, y el elefante, entre otros. Se cree que se han extinguido más de dos terceras partes en el transcurso del tiempo, y esta actividad continuará por varios años más, mientras el hombre no tome conciencia y siempre piense en su comodidad.

NARRADOR: Ahora contesta las preguntas de la 46, 47, y 48.

46. **¿Quiénes han sido los más perjudicados por las malas actuaciones del hombre?**

    A. Los animales.

    B. Todo el ecosistema en general.

    C. La flora y la fauna.

    D. El hombre.

47. **¿Qué especies son las que se encuentran en vía de extinción?**

    A. El orangután, los corales, y las ardillas.

    B. El canguro, el oso polar, y la serpiente.

    C. Los canguros, el tigre de bengala, y el koala.

    D. Las ballenas, las tortugas de mar, y los elefantes.

48. **¿Cuántos animales se han extinguido aproximadamente?**

    A. La cuarta parte de los existentes.

    B. Dos cuartas partes de los que existen.

    C. Dos terceras partes de los animales.

    D. La sexta parte de la actual.

SECTION III

Reading Part A: Discrete Sentences

Directions: The following statements are incomplete, followed by four suggested completions. Select the one that best completes the sentence.

49. ¿Quién _____ pastel de fresa?

    A. tiene

    B. quiera

    C. tengo

    D. quiero

50. ¡_____ ha crecido este niño!

    A. Cómo

    B. Como

    C. Quién

    D. Quien

51. Algunos tés son medicinales como los de menta _____ hierbabuena.

    A. e

    B. y

    C. u

    D. para

52. La mayoría de _____ ducharse en la mañana que en la noche.

    A. las gentes prefieren

    B. la gente prefiere

    C. las gentes prefieren

    D. las gentes prefiere

53. Actualmente, el Sida VIH es catalogada como la _____más grande del mundo.

    A. epidemia

    B. malestar

    C. epidemias

    D. pandemia

54. Mi maestro de inglés se llama _____.

    A. Andres

    B. Angelo

    C. Angela

    D. Ángel

55. La computadora
_____ puede conectar
a la Internet.

A. No sé

B. Nose

C. No se

D. Nosé

56. En mi familia, los adultos
y nosotros los jóvenes, nos
juntamos todos los
domingos a jugar dominó.
Los adultos llevan la
comida y nosotros
_____ los refrescos.

A. compramos

B. comprar

C. compran

D. compraron

57. Enrique y José
_____ durante todo
el día de hoy.

A. ha jugado

B. han jugado

C. hemos jugado

D. he jugado

58. El bebé que está enfrente
de mí apenas tiene seis
meses y está jugando con
un _____ de peluche.

A. oso polar

B. osito

C. sos

D. osote

59. Camila no tiene pasaporte,
ni yo _____.

A. nada

B. nadie

C. también

D. tampoco

60. La señora vende ropa de
_____ colores y tallas.

A. muchas

B. muy

C. muchachas

D. muchos

61. El _____ niño _____ todos sus juguetes con la inundación de la semana pasada.

    A. pobre, pierde

    B. mejor, pobre

    C. pobre, perdió

    D. astuto, pobre

62. Si _____ más, no habría reprobado el examen.

    A. hubiera estudiado

    B. hubiese pensado

    C. he estudiado

    D. hubiésemos estudiado

63. _____ fui a jugar béisbol con mis amigos.

    A. Ayer

    B. La semana pasada

    C. Hoy

    D. Todas las anteriores

64. Tengo ganas de _____ sopa.

    A. comer

    B. beber

    C. tomar

    D. hornear

65. En dos años yo _____ casada y con hijos.

    A. tendré

    B. estaré

    C. estuviera

    D. tuviera

66. Los Olmecas _____ la primera civilización prehispánica de América. Sin embargo, no _____ una civilización tan antigua, la Universidad de Oxford en Inglaterra aún es más.

    A. fue, es

    B. fueron, es

    C. eran, son

    D. es, son

67.   La maestra me dijo que
      podía utilizar el color rojo
      ___ otro que me gustara.

      A. o

      B. ni

      C. u

      D. que

SECTION III

Reading Part B: Short Cloze Passages

Directions: In each of the following paragraphs, there are blanks indicating that words or phrases have been omitted. For each blank, choose the completion that is most appropriate, given the context of the entire paragraph.

I. ___68___ amapolas ___69___ una especie de flores que crecen en Europa, Asia, y Norteamérica. Se pueden ___70___ en diferentes colores. Mis favoritas son las de color blanco ___71___ me transmiten tranquilidad y paz interior.

68.	69.	70.	71.
A. La	A. son	A. buscar	A. por qué
B. El	B. somos	B. hallar	B. por que
C. Las	C. era	C. tener	C. porqué
D. Los	D. tienen	D. crecer	D. porque

II. Felipe siempre ___72___ mi mejor amigo. ___73___ y yo jugamos al fútbol y ___74___ dulces juntos. Una vez, comimos un dulce tan ___75___ que nos provocó dolor de estómago.

72.	73.	74.	75.
A. es	A. el	A. tenemos	A. ha cedo
B. ha sido	B. Él	B. cuidamos	B. ha sido
C. ácido	C. El	C. regalamos	C. ácido
D. acido	D. ella	D. comemos	D. acido

III. La Guerra de los Pasteles fue el primer conflicto ___76___ entre México y Francia. Los ___77___ franceses con negocios establecidos en México, se ___78___ de las rebeliones civiles constantes. En una ocasión ___79___ soldados del ejército de Santa Ana se comieron tres pasteles sin pagar, dando inicio a la «Guerra de los Pasteles».

76.	77.	78.	79.
A. amoroso	A. obreros	A. quejaban	A. ciertos
B. estudiantil	B. dueños	B. quejan	B. siertos
C. bélico	C. abogados	C. queja	C. cientos
D. juvenil	D. maestros	D. quejavan	D. sientos

289

IV. _____80_____ en mi rancho _____81_____ muchas _____82_____
que cuando son molestadas, pican a quien las molesta, haciéndoles
exclamar _____83_____.

80. A. Ahí
B. hay
C. ¡hay!
D. ¡ay!

81. A. Ahí
B. hay
C. ¡hay!
D. ¡ay!

82. A. ovejas
B. abejas
C. avispa
D. avejas

83. A. Ahí
B. hay
C. ¡hay!
D. ¡ay!

V. El director de mi escuela está haciendo una colecta _____84_____ el coro.
Ellos _____85_____ uniformes nuevos _____86_____ pronto irán a un
concurso de canto. Yo quería ayudar, _____87_____ tengo dinero.

84. A. de
B. para
C. a
D. en

85. A. necesitan
B. tienen
C. cosen
D. cocen

86. A. ya que
B. ni
C. pero
D. debido a

87. A. ya que
B pero no
C. y doy
D. debido a

VI. En algunos países latinoamericanos ___88___ tacos y las tortillas
___89___ parte de su historia y son la base de sus _____90_____ desde
las culturas indígenas. Hay gran variedad de tacos que pueden prepararse
con tortillas, siendo los más conocidos ___91___ de carne.

88. A. los
B. las
C. el
D. unos

89. A. forman
B. formaron
C. formarán
D. forma

90. A. alimentos
B. calzados
C. trastes
D. alimento

91. A. la
B. los
C. el
D. uno

SECTION III

Reading Part C: Reading passages & Authentic Stimulus Material

Directions: Read each of the passages below. Each passage is followed by questions or incomplete statements. Choose the best answer according to the text and mark in the corresponding answer.

Archivo Municipal de Saltillo. (1886). Infolios de la Gazeta del Saltillo, Reglas para la vida (airada). Source:
http://www.archivomunicipaldesaltillo.info

92. **¿Qué acción realiza la mujer?**

    A. Tejer.

    B. Coser.

    C. Cocer.

    D. Comer.

Novo, S. (2014). Estrenadores vs conservadores. [Newspaper]. Source:
http://www.archivomunicipaldesaltillo.info

93. **¿Qué se observa en la imagen?**

    A. Sombreros.

    B. Carrera de caballos.

    C. Artículos antiguos.

    D. Un piano.

Limón, N. (2014). Estrategias de autorrepresentación fotográfica, el caso de Frida Kahlo. UC3M Frida Kahlo, Mexican Artist.

94. **¿Qué trae puesto el sujeto?**

    A. Pantalones.

    B. Un abrigo.

    C. Una falda.

    D. Un tutú.

Vanguardia Liberal. (2015). Tom Cruise recorre el país visitando las locaciones de su película "mena". [Newspaper]. Source: http://www.vanguardia.com

95. **¿De qué se trata la noticia?**

    A. De una invitación a una película.

    B. Del rodaje de una película.

    C. Del estreno de una película

    D. De la visita a las locaciones de una película.

96. **¿Cuántos días durará la visita?**

    A. Una quincena.

    B. Hasta enero de 2017.

    C. Nueve días.

    D. Nueve semanas.

Ana es deportista y social. Mónica es callada y prefiere leer un buen libro durante su tiempo libre. Rocío es nadadora y también forma parte del equipo de básquetbol. María quiere ser actriz y bailarina profesional. Karla disfruta escribir poemas y pasar tiempo en la biblioteca.

97. De acuerdo con el párrafo, ¿quiénes podrían llegar a ser mejores amigas en base de sus intereses?

   A. Mónica y Rocío

   B. Rocío y Ana.

   C. Mónica y María.

   D. Karla y María.

La llamativa anémona de mar debe su nombre a la flor anémona. Esta última forma es parte de una familia de 120 especies con formas y colores variados. Procede del Japón y es utilizada comúnmente para el diseño de jardines, las cuales brotan en la primavera.

98. ¿De qué se trata el párrafo?

   A. De las anémonas de mar.

   B. De las anémonas de luz.

   C. De las flores anémona.

   D. De las anémonas del Japón.

La pólvora negra es la mezcla explosiva más antigua, obtenida a base de tres sustancias que por separado están exentas de daño--azufre, carbón vegetal, y salitre. La fecha y circunstancias de su descubrimiento son inciertas todavía. Conocida desde el Siglo XIII, se utilizó para sustituir a los sistemas de propulsión de armas.

99. ¿Cuál debería ser el título del párrafo?

    A. *La historia de la pólvora negra.*

    B. *Cómo hacer pólvora negra.*

    C. *Los ingredientes de la pólvora negra.*

    D. *La pólvora negra y sus usos.*

Albert Einstein no pronunció alguna palabra hasta los dos años de edad. Cuando al fin habló, todo lo repetía dos veces. La mayor parte de su infancia la pasaba solo, jugando principalmente con juguetes mecánicos. En contra de lo que se cree, Einstein no fue un mal estudiante. Al llegar a la edad adulta, era tanta su fama que sólo se rodeaba de celebridades y personas importantes. Se cuenta que en una ocasión Marilyn Monroe le hizo una propuesta ciertamente peculiar, diciéndole que si ellos dos tuvieran hijos y heredaban su genio y la belleza de ella, serían gran personas. A lo que Einstein respondió, «Pero imagínate si ellos heredaran mi belleza y tu inteligencia, nadie los quisiera».

100. ¿Qué mito se desmiente en el párrafo?

    A. Que Einstein era un mal estudiante.

    B. Que Einstein habló hasta ya muy tarde en su vida.

    C. Que Einstein era soltero.

    D. Que Marilyn Monroe le propuso matrimonio.

Cuando hablamos de los objetos, pensamos también en su utilización en los diferentes espacios de la casa, por ejemplo el espacio social, el íntimo y el de los servicios. También la evolución de esos objetos refleja las influencias culturales sucesivas que ha tenido la región. Primero tenemos la entrada de la casa. Antiguamente las ciudades novohispanas no estaban pavimentadas. Había lodo y estiércol en las calles. Antes de pasar al interior había tapetes para que el visitante pudiera quitarse el polvo de los zapatos. Después se le invitaba a pasar.

101. ¿Cuál de las siguientes opciones sustituye la palabra «sucesivas» en la tercera línea?

   A. Siguientes.

   B. Repetidas.

   C. Progresivas.

   D. Continuas.

En el año 3000 antes de Cristo, los chinos descubrieron que los filamentos que cubrían los capullos de los gusanos de seda podían ser tratados y convertidos en tejido. China guardó el secreto de la sericultura hasta el año 300 antes de Cristo. Más tarde, el secreto llegó hasta Corea debido a los tejedores coreanos que trabajaban en China. Japón aprendió a desarrollar la técnica pronto.

Los comerciantes fueron quienes llevaron la seda hasta Europa a través de la ruta de 4,000 millas bautizada como la «Ruta de la Seda».

En Roma, la ley prohibía a los hombres llevar seda porque la consideraban algo demasiado femenino.

Dos monjes persas llevaron gusanos de seda de contrabando hasta Constantinopla en el Siglo VI, y así llegó el arte de la producción de seda hasta Europa, donde floreció hasta la Segunda Guerra Mundial.

La seda sigue siendo un producto de lujo y alto estatus.

102. Sinónimo de la palabra «tratados» en la línea 2:

   A. Convenios.

   B. Acuerdos.

   C. Procesos.

   D. Negociar.

103. ¿Cómo fue que el arte de la producción de seda llegó a Europa?

   A. De contrabando.

   B. Por los comerciantes.

   C. Por la «Ruta de la Seda».

   D. Debido a la Segunda Guerra Mundial.

104. ¿Cuál debería ser el título del párrafo?

   A. China y los gusanos de seda.

   B. La seda en China.

   C. Los contrabandistas persas.

   D. La ley de seda en Roma.

Las lenguas diversas se extinguen con rapidez. De las 7,000 que existen hoy, sólo se hablarán la mitad al finalizar el Siglo XXI. Lenguas como el Uranino; hablado por apenas 3,000 personas en el Amazonas, el Halkomelem; hablado por doscientos en La Canadá y el Tofa; hablado por no más de personas en Siberia, se enfrentan a un futuro incierto.

Los parlantes nativos dejan de utilizar sus lenguas maternas por varios motivos. Tal vez empezaron a utilizar lenguas más dominantes, con más prestigio o más conocidas. Motivados probablemente por las políticas oficiales del Estado para suprimir el idioma o por presión social. Actualmente se fuerza a los niños de todo el mundo para que aprendan las lenguas que predominan hoy día en el planeta. Cuando una lengua muere, se lleva con ella muchas otras cosas, tal como conocimientos únicos acerca del planeta y sus criaturas, un tesoro de mitos y poesía, y una ventana que nos puede ayudar a descifrar el funcionamiento de la mente humana. Los conservacionistas de lenguas trabajan para revivir las lenguas muertas que aún pueden salvarse y documentar aquellas cuya salvación es imposible antes de que desaparezcan para siempre.

~ National Geographic, 2015

105. ¿Qué tipo de texto es?

A. Informativo.

B. Satírico.

C. Poesía.

D. Comparativo.

106. ¿Qué sucede cuando muere una lengua?

A. Se lleva la sabiduría de la cultura que la portaba.

B. Aparecen lenguas estándares nuevas que hablan de criaturas diversas.

C. Es más difícil comprender el funcionamiento de la mente humana.

D. Hay que documentarla antes de que muera para siempre.

El zar y la camisa
1Un zar, hallándose enfermo, dijo:
-¡Daré la mitad de mi reino a quien me cure!
Entonces todos los sabios celebraron una junta para buscar una manera de curar al zar, mas no encontraron medio alguno.
Uno de ellos sin embargo, declaró que era posible curar al zar.
Si sobre la tierra se encuentra un hombre feliz, dijo, quítesele la

camisa y que se la ponga el zar, con lo que éste se curará.

El zar hizo buscar en su reino a un hombre feliz. Los enviados del soberano se esparcieron por todo el reino, mas no pudieron descubrir a un hombre feliz. No encontraron un hombre contento con suerte.

El uno era rico, pero estaba enfermo; el otro gozaba de salud, pero era pobre; aquél, rico y sano, se quejaba de su mujer; aquel otro hombre, de sus hijos. Todos deseaban algo. Cierta noche, muy tarde, el hijo del zar, al pasar frente a una pobre choza, oyó que alguien exclamaba:

Gracias a Dios he trabajado y comido bien. ¿Qué me falta?

El hijo del zar se sintió lleno de alegría; inmediatamente mandó que le llevaran la camisa de aquel hombre, a quien en cambio había de darle cuánto dinero exigiera.

Los enviados se presentaron a toda prisa en la casa de aquel hombre para quitarle la camisa; pero el hombre feliz era tan pobre que no tenía camisa.

~ *León Tolstoi, «El zar y la camisa», 1992*

107. ¿Qué tipo de texto es?

   A. Satírico.

   B. Informativo.

   C. Poema.

   D. Narrativo.

108. ¿Quién se quejaba de sus hijos?

   A. El zar.

   B. El hombre pobre.

   C. El hombre sin camisa

   D. El hombre rico.

109. ¿Cómo está el hombre más feliz del mundo de acuerdo con la historia?

   A. Pobre.

   B. Rico.

   C. Feliz.

   D. Risueño.

110. ¿Quién encontró al hombre más feliz?

   A. El zar.

   B. Los sabios del zar.

   C. El hijo del zar.

   D. Los enviados del zar.

111. ¿Quién es el personaje principal?

   A. El zar.

   B. El hombre sin camisa.

   C. El hijo del zar.

   D. La camisa.

112. ¿Para qué necesitaba el zar una camisa?

   A. Porque no tenía una.

   B. Porque tenía frío.

   C. Para ser feliz.

   D. Para curarse.

113. ¿Cuál es la moraleja de la historia?

   A. El dinero no compra la felicidad.

   B. Las camisas hacen felices a los hombres.

   C. Los hijos siempre son buenos encontrando lo que se les pida.

   D. Padres e hijos deben pasar más tiempo juntos para lograr la felicidad.

Los dioses que adoraban los naturales de esta tierra--la Nueva España

Los aztecas tenían varios dioses que, según sus creencias, intervenían en los asuntos humanos y en algunas ocasiones, hasta los dirigían. Eran dioses celestes y a ellos estaban consagrados los templos.

El dios principal era Huitzilopochtli, el sol, el guerrero eternamente joven, que luchaba contra los demás dioses para que los hombres pudieran vivir. Vencía a la noche y hacía surgir el día nuevo.

El dios de la lluvia, Tláloc, era muy antiguo. Su aparición se remontaba a la época tolteca, 200 A.C. Como tenía el poder sobre la lluvia, a él se le pedía el crecimiento y la vida. En la Tercera Era, Tláloc trajo la luz.

A Quetzalcóatl, la serpiente emplumada, el dios de la sabiduría y del planeta Venus, se le adoraba en distintas configuraciones. Era el señor de la Segunda Era, la de los cuatro vientos, durante la cual el mundo fue devastado por los huracanes y los hombres se convirtieron en monos.

Este dios, llamado Huitzilopochtli, fue robustísimo de grandes fuerzas y muy belicoso-- gran destruidor de pueblos y matador de hombres. En las guerras era como fuego vivo, muy temeroso a sus contrarios y así, la divisa que traía era una cabeza de dragón, que echaba fuego por la boca y era muy espantable. También era ni romántico o embaidor, que se transformaba en figura de aves y bestias diversas.

Este dios, llamado Páinal, era como sota capitán, porque el arribo dicho, como mayor capitán, dictaba cuándo se había de hacer guerra a algunas provincias. Éste, como su vicario, sería para cuando repentinamente se ofrecía salir al encuentro de los enemigos, porque entonces era menester que este Páinal, que quiere decir «ligero», «apresurado», salía en persona a mover a la gente para que con toda prisa salieran a haberse con los enemigos.

El dios llamado Tezcatlipoca era tenido por verdadero dios e invisible, el cual andaba en todo lugar--en el cielo, en la tierra, y en el infierno. Y tenían que, cuando andaba en la tierra, movía guerras, enemistades, y discordias de donde surgían fatigas y desasosiegos.

Decían que él mismo incitaba a unos contra otros para que tuvieran guerras y por esto le llamaban Nécoc Yáotl, que significa «sembrador de discordias de ambas partes». Y decían que sólo él entendía el regimiento del mundo y que sólo él daba las prosperidades y riquezas y que, solamente él, las quitaba cuando se le antojaba. Daba riquezas, prosperidades y fama y fortaleza y señoríos y dignidades y honras y las quitaba cuando se le antojaba.

Este dios Tláloc Tlamacazqui, era el dios de las lluvias. Lo tenían por el que daba las lluvias para que se regaran las tierras, mediante la cual se criaban todas las hierbas, árboles, frutas, y mantenimientos. También le tenían por el que enviaba el granizo, los relámpagos, y los rayos, las tempestades del agua así como los peligros de los ríos y del mar.

El nombre, Tláloc Tlamacazqui quiere decir que es dios que habita en el paraíso terrenal y que otorga a los hombres lo necesario para el mantenimiento de la vida corporal.

~ Fray Bernardino de Sahagún, Narraciones Históricas, 1590.

114. ¿Cuál es el tema principal del texto?

A. La religión Azteca.

B. Las memorias de Fray Bernardino de Sahagún.

C. Huitzilopochtli.

D. Tláloc Tlamacazqui.

115. ¿Cuál pudiera ser un título alterno al actual?

A. *Las aventuras de los Dioses en la Nueva España.*

B. *Los poderes de los Dioses Divinos.*

C. *Los Dioses del Olimpo en la Nueva España.*

D. *Los Dioses Aztecas y sus encomiendas respectivas.*

116. ¿Qué tipo de texto es?

A. Texto informativo.

B. Texto literario.

C. Texto histórico.

D. Texto narrativo.

117. ¿A qué se refiere la frase «a haberse» en la línea 23?

A. A encontrarse.

B. A verse.

C. A tenerse.

D. A buscarse.

118. ¿Qué error de redacción se observa en la línea 33?

A. No hay concordancia en el texto.

B. La palabra, «fortaleza» se escribe con «s», «fortalesa»

C. Se repite la letra «y».

D. Faltan comas.

119. ¿A qué se refiere la frase, «se criaban todas las hierbas»" en la línea 36?

A. Había que educar a las hierbas.

B. Las hierbas eran cultivadas.

C. Había que podar las hierbas.

D. Todas las hierbas crecían por doquier.

120. ¿Cuál de los dioses era grande físicamente?

A. Tláloc Tlamacazqui.

B. Huitzilopochtli.

C. Quetzalcóatl.

D. Páinal.

SPANISH LANGUAGE

ANSWER KEY

Question Number	Correct Answer	Your Answer	Question Number	Correct Answer	Your Answer	Question Number	Correct Answer	Your Answer
1.	D		41.	D		81.	B	
2.	D		42.	B		82.	B	
3.	D		43.	C		83.	D	
4.	C		44.	B		84.	B	
5.	C		45.	B		85.	A	
6.	A		46.	B		86.	A	
7.	B		47.	D		87.	B	
8.	B		48.	C		88.	A	
9.	C		49.	A		89.	A	
10.	C		50.	A		90.	A	
11.	C		51.	B		91.	B	
12.	A		52.	B		92.	B	
13.	A		53.	D		93.	C	
14.	B		54.	D		94.	C	
15.	A		55.	C		95.	D	
16.	B		56.	A		96.	C	
17.	B		57.	B		97.	B	
18.	D		58.	B		98.	C	
19.	C		59.	D		99.	A	
20.	B		60.	D		100.	A	
21.	B		61.	C		101.	D	
22.	D		62.	A		102.	C	
23.	A		63.	D		103.	A	
24.	A		64.	A		104.	B	
25.	B		65.	B		105.	A	
26.	B		66.	B		106.	A	
27.	C		67.	C		107.	A	
28.	C		68.	C		108.	B	
29.	D		69.	A		109.	A	
30.	B		70.	B		110.	C	
31.	B		71.	D		111.	A	
32.	D		72.	B		112.	D	
33.	A		73.	B		113.	A	
34.	B		74.	D		114.	A	
35.	C		75.	C		115.	D	
36.	A		76.	C		116.	C	
37.	A		77.	B		117.	A	
38.	C		78.	A		118.	C	
39.	C		79.	A		119.	B	
40.	B		80.	A		120.	B	

RATIONALES

19.   ¿Cuál fue el motivo por el cual Juan visitó el banco?

>   A.   Fue a modificar su número de identificación porque estaba incorrecto.

>   B.   Fue a reclamar un dinero que le consignaron.

>   C.   Fue a cambiar un cheque.

>   D.   Fue a hablar con el director del banco porque estaba confundido.

La respuesta correcta es la C
La respuesta correcta es la C porque Juan fue al banco a cambiar un cheque bancario.

20.   ¿Por qué le negaron el cambio del cheque bancario a Juan?

>   A.   Porque el valor del cheque superaba los cinco mil dólares.

>   B.   Porque Juan era menor de edad y la ley lo prohibía.

>   C.   Porque el cheque no tenía fecha.

>   D.   Porque Juan no presentó su número de identificación.

La respuesta correcta es la B
La respuesta correcta es la B, porque a pesar de que Juan tenía tarjeta de identificación él era menor de edad.

21.   ¿Qué tuvo que hacer Juan para que le cambiarán el cheque bancario?

A.   Tuvo que hacer unas llamadas a la sucursal principal.

B.   Tuvo que hablar con el director del banco.

C.   Tuvo que pedir unas autorizaciones por parte de la empresa donde trabajaba.

D.   Tuvo que esperar al gerente de la empresa donde él trabajaba por media hora, para que le autorizara su cheque.

La respuesta correcta es la B
La respuesta correcta es la B, porque él espero media hora al Gerente del Banco para hablar con él.

22.   ¿Qué estaba haciendo Sergio en la biblioteca?

A.   Estaba leyendo el libro, «Fundamentos de Economía».

B.   Estaba estudiando para una prueba de economía.

C.   Estaba leyendo la biografía de Edmund Burke.

D.   Prestó un libro de Edmund Burke.

La respuesta correcta es la D
La respuesta correcta es la D, porque el prestó un libro de fundamentos de economía cuyo autor era Edmund Burke.

23.   ¿Cuánto tiempo le prestarán el libro a Sergio?

A.   Dos semanas.

B.   Una semana.

C.   Mes y medio.

D.   Cincuenta días.

La respuesta correcta es la A
La respuesta correcta es la A, porque el libro sólo se lo prestarán 15 días

24. **¿Qué sucede si Sergio no entrega el libro a la biblioteca en el tiempo estipulado?**

    A. La biblioteca le privará los servicios a Sergio.

    B. Le cobrarán el libro como nuevo.

    C. Lo reportan con la biblioteca.

    D. Debe asistir a unas conferencias de capacitación y concientización

La respuesta correcta es la A
La respuesta correcta es la A, porque la biblioteca no le volvería a prestar libros a Sergio.

25. **¿Qué harán Edwin y Martha en el zoológico?**

    A. Harán un recorrido por todo el zoológico.

    B. Conocerán a un animal en específico.

    C. Participarán de una muestra de animales salvajes.

    D. Atenderán una serie de recomendaciones por parte del zoológico.

La respuesta correcta es la B
La respuesta correcta es la B, porque Edwin le mostrará el Búfalo

26. **Según lo que le planteó Edwin a Martha, el animal que narran ¿es furioso?**

    A. Sí, porque embiste sin alguna discriminación.

    B. No, pero si se altera en momentos de peligro.

    C. Sí, porque cuando ve personas, se altera demasiado.

    D. No, porque por naturaleza del búfalo es furioso.

La respuesta correcta es la B
La respuesta correcta es la B, porque el Búfalo solo se altera cuando se encuentra en situaciones de peligro.

27. **¿Qué tuvo que hacer Martha cuando se fue del zoológico?**

    A. Pagar su estadía en el zoológico.

    B. Confirmar su asistencia para la próxima visita.

    C. Consignar su nombre en la recepción del zoológico.

    D. Registrar la huella en el lector

La respuesta correcta es la C
La respuesta correcta es la C, porque Martha tuvo que registrar su nombre en la entrada del zoológico.

28. **¿Qué le pidió Laura a Erika?**

    A. Dos máquinas selladoras para cerrar unas pacas.

    B. Un informe para el departamento de mantenimiento.

    C. Los reportes de producción sobre las pacas empacadas.

    D. La producción de los últimos días.

La respuesta correcta es C
La respuesta correcta es C, porque Erika tenía que pasarle a Laura los informes de producción de las pacas.

29. **Al final de cuentas, ¿cuántas pacas se empacaron en total?**

    A. Trescientas pacas de bombón, cien de chicle y doscientas de menta.

    B. Cien de menta, doscientas de bombón y trescientas de chicle.

    C. Doscientas de chicle, trescientas de menta y cien de bombón.

    D. Seiscientas pacas de todos los productos.

La respuesta correcta es la D
La respuesta correcta es la D, porque la pregunta hace referencia al total de todos los productos, no de cada uno.

30. ¿Últimamente por qué está recibiendo Laura quejas de los clientes?

    A. Porque no están cumpliendo con el número de pedidos.

    B. Porque no están respetando los tiempos de entrega.

    C. Porque están entregando productos de mala calidad.

    D. Porque los productos están muy costosos.

La respuesta correcta es la B

La respuesta correcta es la B, porque la empresa no está cumpliendo con los tiempos de entrega.

31. De acuerdo con la narración, el profesor :

    A. Dictará la clase explicando todo el tema de la termodinámica.

    B. Aclarará las dudas relacionadas con el tema.

    C. Entregará los exámenes de la termodinámica y resolverá las dudas del mismo.

    D. Preparará el examen de la termodinámica.

La respuesta correcta es la B

La respuesta correcta es la B, ya que el profesor dedicará el tiempo a aclarar las dudas del tema en mención.

32.   ¿A qué hace referencia la expresión, «el tiempo corre y las horas vuelan»?

    A.   La clase es muy corta y el profesor debe responder rápidamente a las dudas.

    B.   Las dudas deben preguntarlas rápidamente porque el profesor tiene mucho afán.

    C.   Las dudas deben ser muy concisas porque el profesor cuenta con poco tiempo.

    D.   El tiempo pasa rápidamente y el profesor sólo cuenta con una hora para responder a las dudas.

La respuesta correcta es la D
La respuesta correcta es la D, porque esta expresión es muy común cuando una persona se va a referir a que el tiempo pasa muy rápido.

33.   ¿En qué campo es importante la variable, «tiempo»?

    A.   En la industria, porque gracias a él, se establece si un proceso químico es viable o no.

    B.   En las investigaciones científicas, ya que con esta variable se sabe cuánto dura una reacción.

    C.   En los laboratorios, porque con el tiempo se analiza la caducidad de una reacción.

    D.   En ventas, ya que con esta variable se determinan si éstas son rentables o no.

La respuesta correcta es la A
La respuesta correcta es la A, porque en la narración mencionan que esta variable se utiliza en la industria para determinar si un proceso químico es rentable o no.

34. **Algunas partes de la historia del ser humano son:**

    A. Modificadas e inconclusas.

    B. Ambiguas y desconocidas.

    C. Imprecisas y confusas.

    D. Complejas y desconocidas.

La respuesta correcta es la B
La respuesta correcta es la B, ya que la palabra es sinónimo de confuso.

35. **Las teorías que los científicos han expuesto a los seres humanos:**

    A. Son tan convincentes, que las personas creen plenamente en ellas.

    B. Generan dudas, ya que no están apoyados en testimonios reales.

    C. Están bien soportadas, pero aún no logran persuadir.

    D. No son verídicas porque no se han apoyado en testimonios reales.

La respuesta correcta es la C
La respuesta correcta es la C, porque esta afirmación es la que narran en el texto a pesar de que se nombra diferente.

36. **¿De qué depende el ser humano para sobrevivir?**

    A. De su entorno y del medio ambiente.

    B. De sus propios esfuerzos.

    C. Del dinero que gana por su trabajo.

    D. Del medio ambiente y de sí mismo.

La respuesta correcta es la A
La respuesta correcta es la A, porque en la narración mencionan que estas dos variables.

37. ¿Cuál es el aspecto más grave que han provocado las enfermedades en las personas?

   A. Las alteraciones emocionales.

   B. Los descuidos en el cuidado de su salud.

   C. La falta de dinero para acudir al doctor.

   D. El sedentarismo.

La respuesta correcta es la A
La respuesta correcta es la A, porque las emociones han sido la principal causa de las enfermedades de las personas.

38. ¿Por qué ha marcado la diferencia la programación neurolingüística en los últimos tiempos?

   A. Porque ha sido una de las terapias más innovadoras.

   B. Porque utiliza tecnología de punta para tratar a los pacientes.

   C. Porque le ha cambiado la vida a miles de personas debido a sus tratamientos.

   D. Porque sus creadores son científicos bastante creativos.

La respuesta correcta es la C
La respuesta correcta es la C, porque la PNL ha sido muy efectiva en el tratamiento de diversos trastornos.

39.   **La programación neurolingüística:**

A.   Ayuda en curar enfermedades pero no resuelve la auto-dependencia.

B.   Ayuda en mejorar los hábitos malos y a ser exitoso.

C.   Logra que una persona se auto-motive por sí misma.

D.   Logra que una persona pierda los miedos, pero no por un largo periodo.

La respuesta correcta es la C

La respuesta correcta es la C, porque en la narración lo mencionan muy claramente.

40.   **¿Cuántas personas mueren al año por causa del cigarrillo tradicional?**

A.   Seiscientos mil de personas.

B.   Seis millones de personas.

C.   Seis mil personas.

D.   Sesenta mil personas.

La respuesta correcta es la B

La respuesta correcta es la B, porque es la cifra de personas que mueren al año por causa del cigarrillo.

41.   ¿Es buena para la salud el cigarrillo electrónico?

    A.   No, porque genera dependencia a la nicotina.

    B.   No, porque genera problemas cardiovasculares.

    C.   Sí, porque ayuda en eliminar la dependencia con la nicotina.

    D.   Es ambiguo porque existen opiniones divididas.

La respuesta correcta es la D
La respuesta correcta es la D, porque en la narración existen opiniones divididas acerca del cigarrillo electrónico.

42.   ¿A qué invita la narración?

    A.   A que no fumen las personas porque sus consecuencias no son irreversibles.

    B.   A informar sobre el riesgo del cigarrillo tradicional y del cigarrillo electrónico.

    C.   A discutir sobre los usos del cigarrillo.

    D.   A armar huelgas para que cierren las tabaqueras.

La respuesta correcta es la B
La respuesta correcta es la B, porque este tipo de narraciones son informativas.

43.   ¿Qué ha ocurrido con la economía de los países en los últimos años?

A.   Algunos se han visto afectados fuertemente por la crisis económica mundial.

B.   Las economías tercermundistas han entrado en un proceso de expansión.

C.   Algunas economías han mejorado pero otras han entrado en crisis.

D.   Ha provocado muchas crisis internas.

La respuesta correcta es la C
La respuesta correcta es la C, porque la economía ha generado desequilibrios, unos países han mejorado y otros están desmejorando cada día.

44.   ¿Qué ha afectado a la economía?

A.   Los problemas políticos y las diferencias sociales.

B.   Los problemas ambientales y desigualdades.

C.   La burocracia.

D.   Los conflictos internos y externos de los países.

La respuesta correcta es la B
La respuesta correcta es la B, porque inequidad es igual a desigualdad.

45.   ¿Qué se debe hacer para que la economía se pueda mejorar?

A.   Los gobiernos se deben comprometer a generar más empleo.

B.   Se debe hacer una reestructuración del modelo económico.

C.   Se deben generar oportunidades nuevas en el modelo social.

D.   Ninguna de las anteriores.

La respuesta correcta es la B
La respuesta correcta es la B, porque se plantea que se reestructure el modelo económico para generar nuevas oportunidades.

46. ¿Quiénes han sido los más perjudicados por las malas actuaciones del hombre?

   A. Los animales.

   B. Todo el ecosistema en general.

   C. La flora y la fauna.

   D. El hombre.

La respuesta correcta es la B

La respuesta correcta es la B, porque el hombre ha perjudicado a todo el medio ambiente.

47. ¿Qué especies son las que se encuentran en vía de extinción?

   A. El orangután, los corales, y las ardillas.

   B. El canguro, el oso polar, y la serpiente.

   C. Los canguros, el tigre de bengala, y el koala.

   D. Las ballenas, las tortugas de mar, y los elefantes.

La respuesta correcta es la D

La respuesta correcta es la D, ya que son las que narran en el texto.

48. ¿Cuántos animales se han extinguido aproximadamente?

   A. La cuarta parte de los existentes.

   B. Dos cuartas partes de los que existen.

   C. Dos terceras partes de los animales.

   D. La sexta parte de la actual.

La respuesta correcta es la C

La respuesta correcta es la C, ya que es la cifra aproximada de los animales que se han extinguido.

49.   ¿Quién _____ pastel de fresa?

    A.   tiene

    B.   quiera

    C.   tengo

    D.   quiero

La respuesta correcta es A
Al no encontrarse escrito un sujeto como tal, el verbo "quiere" cumple la función de sujeto tácito, es decir, cuando el sujeto está implícito en el contexto de la oración.

50.   ¡_____ ha crecido este niño!

    A.   Cómo

    B.   Como

    C.   Quién

    D.   Quien

La respuesta correcta es A
La palabra "cómo" es tónica y lleva tilde diacrítica cuando tiene sentido interrogativo y exclamativo. La palabra "como" no lleva tilde diacrítica cuando funciona como verbo o comparativo.

51.   Algunos tés son medicinales como los de menta _____ hierbabuena.

    A.   e

    B.   y

    C.   u

    D.   para

La respuesta correcta es B
La conjunción "e" se utiliza cuando la siguiente palabra comienza por "i" o "hi". Sin embargo, no debe usarse ante el diptongo "hie".

52. La mayoría de _____ ducharse en la mañana que en la noche.

    A. las gentes prefieren

    B. la gente prefiere

    C. las gentes prefieren

    D. las gentes prefiere

La respuesta correcta es B
Es la única de las opciones en la que aparece el sujeto colectivo "la gente" escrito de manera correcta. Los sustantivos colectivos son aquellos que, en singular, designan un conjunto de seres pertenecientes a una misma clase. Cuando este tipo de sustantivos funciona como sujeto, el verbo debe ir en singular así como los pronombres, adjetivos y artículos a él referidos.

53. Actualmente, el Sida VIH es catalogada como la _____ más grande del mundo.

    A. epidemia

    B. malestar

    C. epidemias

    D. pandemia

La respuesta correcta es D
Al revisar las opciones encontramos que todas son relativas a enfermedades. En la parte en que se lee "del mundo" se puede deducir que la mejor respuesta es D "pandemia". A diferencia de la epidemia, observamos que el prefijo "pan" en la palabra "pandemia" significa "todo", englobando a "todo el mundo" y no solo una parte de la población, como sería el caso de una epidemia.

54. Mi maestro de inglés se llama _____.

A. Andres

B. Angelo

C. Angela

D. Ángel

La respuesta correcta es D
La regla indica que todas las letras mayúsculas se acentúan, tanto si se trata de palabras escritas en su totalidad con mayúsculas como si se trata únicamente de la mayúscula inicial. La excepción a la regla es si las mayúsculas forman parte de siglas.

55. La computadora _____ puede conectar a la Internet.

A. No sé

B. Nose

C. No se

D. Nosé

La respuesta correcta es C
La oración indica que la palabra "se" funciona como pronombre. Las opciones B y D son incorrectas mientras que la opción A es la negación de la primera persona del singular del verbo "saber".

56. En mi familia, los adultos y nosotros los jóvenes, nos juntamos todos los domingos a jugar dominó. Los adultos llevan la comida y nosotros _____ los refrescos.

   A. compramos

   B. comprar

   C. compran

   D. compraron

La respuesta correcta es A
La opción A corresponde a la correcta conjugación del verbo regular "comprar", en segunda persona del plural. Por lo que "nosotros compramos" es la respuesta correcta.

57. Enrique y José _____ durante todo el día de hoy.

   A. ha jugado

   B. han jugado

   C. hemos jugado

   D. he jugado

La respuesta correcta es B
La conjugación correcta del verbo "jugar" es "han jugado" ya que se indica la tercera persona del plural al mencionarse 2 sustantivos. La preposición "durante" señala que la mejor respuesta debe escribirse en tiempo perfecto y el complemento circunstancial de tiempo "de hoy" señala que se trata del tiempo presente.

58. El bebé que está enfrente de mí apenas tiene seis meses y está jugando con un _____ de peluche.

A. oso polar

B. osito

C. sos

D. osote

La respuesta correcta es B
La opción B sugiere el uso del diminutivo de la palabra "oso". Al indicarse que el sujeto es un bebé, se infiere que dicho sujeto es pequeño, por lo que lo lógico es que esté jugando con un "osito", acorde a su tamaño. De ahí que la opción D se elimina ya que indica el aumentativo de la palabra "oso". La opción A, sugiere que el sujeto esté jugando con un animal salvaje y la opción C refiere una señal de auxilio. Por lo que las opciones A, C y D son incorrectas.

59. Camila no tiene pasaporte, ni yo _____.

A. nada

B. nadie

C. también

D. tampoco

La respuesta correcta es D
"Tampoco" es un adverbio de negación que se utiliza tras otra negación. Definición opuesta a su antónimo "también". Ya que "Camila no tiene pasaporte", y la opción C corresponde a un adverbio afirmativo, la opción C se descarta. Las opciones A y B carecen de lógica sintáctica en la oración, por lo que se eliminan. Dejando la opción D como la mejor respuesta posible.

60. **La señora vende ropa de _____ colores y tallas.**

    A. muchas

    B. muy

    C. muchachas

    D. muchos

La respuesta correcta es D
La opción D sugiere el masculino en plural del adverbio "mucho", mismo que se encuentra definido por los sustantivos "colores" y "tallas". Debido a que la opción A está en femenino, la opción B es un adverbio que intensifica y la opción C se refiere a un sustantivo en plural, la mejor respuesta posible es la opción D.

61. **El _____ niño _____ todos sus juguetes con la inundación de la semana pasada.**

    A. pobre, pierde

    B. mejor, pobre

    C. pobre, perdió

    D. astuto, pobre

La respuesta correcta es C
La regla general establece que el adjetivo se coloca después del sustantivo. Sin embargo, existen algunas excepciones en las que se antepone, mismas que cambian el significado de la oración. En este caso, lo común hubiese sido escribir "El niño pobre", eso indicaría que el niño es pobre económicamente hablando. Al anteponer el adjetivo al sustantivo "El pobre niño", eso indica pobreza moral. El predicado de la oración indica que se habla de pobreza moral.
El complemento circunstancial de tiempo "la semana pasada" indica que el verbo debe ir en pasado simple. Por lo que la opción C es la correcta.

62.   Si _____ más, no habría reprobado el examen.

    A.   hubiera estudiado

    B.   hubiese pensado

    C.   he estudiado

    D.   hubiésemos estudiado

La respuesta correcta es A

El condicional "Si" sugiere que la oración requiere de un verbo en pretérito perfecto. Generalmente, dicha estructura gramatical, se utiliza para generar hipótesis y un posible resultado imaginario en base en acciones en el pasado que no sucedieron.

Nótese que el verbo "habría reprobado" indica que el sujeto se encuentra en primera persona del singular. A partir de las premisas antes mencionadas se pueden descartar las opciones C y D. Dejando así A y B como posibles respuestas. Siendo A la mejor respuesta basado en el contexto de la oración.

63.   _____ fui a jugar béisbol con mis amigos.

    A.   Ayer

    B.   La semana pasada

    C.   Hoy

    D.   Todas las anteriores

La respuesta correcta es D

Todas las opciones son correctas. El verbo "fui" indica tiempo pasado. Los complementos circunstanciales de tiempo "Ayer" y "La semana pasada" indican directamente tiempo pretérito. El complemento circunstancial de tiempo "Hoy" indica indirectamente tiempo pretérito, ya que la acción puede ocurrir el día de hoy en una hora previa a la que la oración indica.

64.   Tengo ganas de _____ sopa.

   A.   comer

   B.   beber

   C.   tomar

   D.   hornear

La respuesta correcta es A
"La sopa" se come, aún y cuando es un platillo que se presenta de forma líquida, no es común "beberla" o "tomarla". Aún y cuando "beberla", "tomarla" o "comerla" son correctos, no es común utilizar los dos primeros.

65.   En dos años yo _____ casada y con hijos.

   A.   tendré

   B.   estaré

   C.   estuviera

   D.   tuviera

La respuesta correcta es B
La parte de la oración "En dos años" indica tiempo futuro, por lo que las opciones C y D se eliminan. Dejando así las opciones A y B como posibles. Sin embargo, el futuro del verbo "estar" complementa la oración adecuadamente.

66. Los Olmecas _____ la primera civilización prehispánica de América. Sin embargo, no _____ una civilización tan antigua, la Universidad de Oxford en Inglaterra aún es más.

    A. fue, es

    B. fueron, es

    C. eran, son

    D. es, son

La respuesta correcta es B
"Los Olmecas" indican que el sujeto es plural por lo que siguiendo las reglas de concordancia nominal, la conjugación correcta del verbo deberá ser en plural aun y cuando le sigue otro sujeto "civilización" la cual es colectiva y por ende le debe anteceder un verbo en singular, se toma el verbo en plural como correcto debido a que "Los Olmecas" es un sustantivo específico y de mayor relevancia que el sustantivo "civilización", el cual es general. Se está hablando principalmente de "Los Olmecas", siendo este el sustantivo dominante, mientras que el sustantivo "civilización" es subdominante.
Por otra parte, en la segunda parte de la oración, el sujeto dominante es "civilización" al cual debe antecederle un verbo en singular. Siguiendo así, la regla que dicta que a un sustantivo cuando es un nombre colectivo y está en singular, el verbo se ha de poner en el mismo número.
Al analizar la oración se observa que la conjugación de los verbos que mejor la complementa es, la conjugación en tiempo pasado. Por lo que la mejor respuesta es B.

67. La maestra me dijo que podía utilizar el color rojo ___ otro que me gustara.

   A. o

   B. ni

   C. u

   D. que

La respuesta correcta es C
Las conjunciones disyuntivas, "o" y "u" indican alternativa. Ya que la palabra que le precede comienza con la letra "o", lo correcto fonética y gramaticalmente es utilizar la conjunción "u".

I. ___68___ amapolas ___69___ una especie de flores que crecen en Europa, Asia, y Norteamérica. Se pueden ___70___ en diferentes colores. Mis favoritas son las de color blanco ___71___ me transmiten tranquilidad y paz interior.

68.	69.	70.	71.
A. La	A. son	A. buscar	A. por qué
B. El	B. somos	B. hallar	B. por que
C. Las	C. era	C. tener	C. porqué
D. Los	D. tienen	D. crecer	D. porque

68. La respuesta correcta es C.
La regla establece que el sustantivo es plural y femenino; así que requiere un artículo plural y femenino, cual en las opciones el único es «Las».

69. La respuesta correcta es A.
Simplemente porque la regla establece que el sustantivo usado en tercera persona es plural y requiere tal tipo de verbo, cual en las opciones el único de ese tipo es «son».

70. La respuesta correcta es B.

Aunque todas las opciones están dentro la regla que requiere que el sustantivo usado en tercera persona, siendo plural lleve tal tipo de verbo, según el tema del texto, «hallar» es la respuesta más apropiada.

71. La respuesta correcta es D.

La razón es porque según el texto se necesita una conjunción para completar la oración. La oración no es presentada como pregunta, así que no requiere acento sobre la «e». La opción (B) divide la conjunción que resulta en deletreo incorrecto. La opción (D) no divide la conjunción, así que es la respuesta correcta.

II. Felipe siempre _____72_____ mi mejor amigo. _____73_____ y yo jugamos al fútbol y _____74_____ dulces juntos. Una vez, comimos un dulce tan _____75_____ que nos provocó dolor de estómago.

72.		73.		74.		75.	
A.	es	A.	el	A.	tenemos	A.	ha cedo
B.	ha sido	B.	Él	B.	cuidamos	B.	ha sido
C.	ácido	C.	El	C.	regalamos	C.	ácido
D.	acido	D.	ella	D.	comemos	D.	acido

72. La respuesta correcta es B.

La oración necesita un verbo, y el adverbio «siempre» indica una temporada extendida o de toda la vida, así que «ha sido» es la respuesta correcta. El verbo «es» que ofrece la opción (A) sólo indica el presente —no todo tiempo, ni toda la vida, así que no es correcto. La opción (C) con la palabra, «ácido», aunque deletreada bien no es correcta, y la opción (D) sólo trata de ofrecer la misma palabra («ácido») deletreada incorrectamente sin acento sobre la «a».

73. La respuesta correcta es B.

La razón es porque el texto se refiere a Felipe, y necesita un pronombre que empiece con letra mayúscula, ya que empieza la oración. La respuesta (A) ofrece «el» sin letra mayúscula y sin acento para indicar pronombre. Aunque la respuesta (C) ofrece «El», en letra mayúscula, no tiene acento sobre la «E» para indicar que es pronombre. La respuesta (D) aunque es pronombre (ella), es femenino y no se puede aplicar al nombre masculino, Felipe.

74. La respuesta correcta es D.
La razón es porque como la oración se trata de sustantivos plurales, necesita un verbo plural en el presente. Aunque todas las opciones consisten de verbos plurales, la opción correcta es la (D) porque según al concluirse el texto, la opción (D) siendo la más relacionada al tema, es la más correcta.

75. La respuesta correcta es C.
La respuesta necesita un verbo singular para completar la oración. La respuesta correcta es (B) porque la respuesta (A) sólo es deletreo incorrecto del verbo «ha sido», deletreándolo como «ha sedo». La respuesta (C) sólo ofrece un sustantivo (ácido) que suena semejante al verbo correcto, «ha sido», y la respuesta (D) ofrece el mismo sustantivo deletreado incorrectamente sin acento (acido).

III.La Guerra de los Pasteles fue el primer conflicto ____76____ entre México y Francia. Los ____77____ franceses con negocios establecidos en México, se ____78____ de las rebeliones civiles constantes. En una ocasión ____79____ soldados del ejército de Santa Ana se comieron tres pasteles sin pagar, dando inicio a la «Guerra de los Pasteles».

76.	A. amoroso	**77.**	A. obreros	**78.**	A. quejaban	**79.**	A. ciertos
	B. estudiantil		B. dueños		B. quejan		B. siertos
	C. bélico		C. abogados		C. queja		C. cientos
	D. juvenil		D. maestros		D. quejavan		D. sientos

76. La respuesta correcta es C.
La oración necesita un adjetivo, y aunque todas las opciones ofrecen uno, la respuesta correcta es (C), porque el tema del texto se trata de guerra.

77. La respuesta correcta es B.
Según el tema de la oración, la respuesta correcta es (B).

78. La respuesta correcta es A.
La oración necesita un verbo plural en el pasado y la única opción disponible de ese tipo sólo es disponible por medio de la respuesta (A). (B) no es correcta porque es verbo en el presente, la respuesta (C) es palabra sustantiva y no califica, y la respuesta (D) sólo es deletreo de la respuesta correcta, el verbo plural correcto (quejaban).

79. La respuesta correcta es A.

La razón es porque el sustantivo masculino plural «soldados» necesita adjetivo masculino plural y «ciertos» es la única respuesta apropiada, y la respuesta (B) ofrece la misma respuesta deletreada incorrectamente. Según el texto, los soldados sólo se comieron tres pasteles. No se comieron cien pasteles. Así que la respuesta (C) es incorrecta, y además de no ser correcta, la respuesta (D) esta deletreada incorrectamente.

IV. ____80____ en mi rancho ____81____ muchas ____82____ que cuando son molestadas, pican a quien las molesta, haciéndoles exclamar ____83____.

80. A. Ahí	**81.** A. Ahí	**82.** A. ovejas	**83.** A. Ahí
B. hay	B. hay	B. abejas	B. hay
C. ¡hay!	C. hay!	C.avispa	C. ¡hay!
D. ¡ay!	D. ¡ay!	D.avejas	D. ¡ay!

80. La respuesta correcta es A.

La razón es porque la oración necesita un adverbio para describir donde está situado el rancho. La respuesta (B) es verbo y no es correcta, La respuesta (C) es verbo e incluye signos de exclamación y por esas razones no califica, y la respuesta (D) es interjección y no es correcta tampoco.

81. La respuesta correcta es B.

La oración necesita un verbo. La respuesta (A) es adverbio y no califica. La respuesta (C) aunque sea el verbo correcto, incluye signos de exclamación y por eso no es correcta. La respuesta (D) es interjección y no es correcta tampoco.

82. La respuesta correcta es B.

La oración necesita un sustantivo plural femenino, y la única respuesta correcta es la (B), porque aunque la respuesta (A) sea sustantivo femenino se refiere a animales tranquilos. La respuesta (C) es singular y por esa razón no califica, y la palabra que ofrece la respuesta (D) no existe.

83. La respuesta correcta es D.

El fin de la oración necesita una interjección exclamatoria, y por esa razón, además que según que el texto indica dolor, la respuesta correcta es la (D). La respuesta (A) es adverbio y no califica. La respuesta (B) es verbo y no califica, y aunque incluye signos de exclamación, la respuesta (C) es verbo y no es correcta.

V. **El director de mi escuela está haciendo una colecta _____84_____ el coro. Ellos _____85_____ uniformes nuevos _____86_____ pronto irán a un concurso de canto. Yo quería ayudar, _____87_____ tengo dinero.**

84.		85.		86.		87.	
A.	de	A.	necesitan	A.	ya que	A.	ya que
B.	para	B.	tienen	B.	ni	B	pero no
C.	a	C.	cosen	C.	pero	C.	y doy
D.	en	D.	cocen	D.	debido a	D.	debido a

84. La respuesta correcta es B.

Se necesita una preposición para completar la frase prepositiva. Ya que la oración se trata de una colecta, la respuesta correcta es (B). Por esa razón, las otras respuestas (A), (C), y (D), aunque son preposiciones no son las más apropiadas para esta oración.

85. La respuesta correcta es A.

El sustantivo plural necesita un verbo plural para completar la oración. Según el tema del texto, la respuesta correcta es (A). Aunque las otras respuestas: Según el tema del texto, la respuesta (B) no es correcta. Según el tema del texto, la respuesta (C) no es correcta tampoco por que el texto no indica que los miembros del coro cosen uniformes. Y la respuesta (D) no es correcta tampoco, porque realmente los uniformes no se deben coser.

86. La respuesta correcta es A.

La oración necesita una conjunción, y aunque las respuestas (B), (C), y (D) contienen conjunciones, según el tema del texto la respuesta (A) es la más correcta.

87. La respuesta correcta es B.

La respuesta necesita una interjección para completar la oración. Según el tema, la respuesta correcta es (B).

VI. En algunos países latinoamericanos ___88__ tacos y las tortillas ___89____ parte de su historia y son la base de sus _____90_____ desde las culturas indígenas. Hay gran variedad de tacos que pueden prepararse con tortillas, siendo los más conocidos __91___ de carne.

88.	A. los	89. A. forman	90. A. alimentos	91. A. la
	B. las	B. formaron	B. calzados	B. los
	C. el	C. formarán	C. trastes	C. el
	D. unos	D. forma	D. alimento	D. uno

88. La respuesta correcta es A.
La oración necesita un artículo plural masculino definitivo, y la respuesta (A) lo provee. La respuesta (B) es femenina y plural y no califica. La respuesta (C) es masculino y singular y no califica, y la respuesta (D) es pronombre masculino plural y no califica.

89. La respuesta correcta es A.
La oración necesita un verbo plural en el presente. La respuesta (A) lo provee. La respuesta (B) provee un verbo plural en el pasado que no califica. La respuesta (C) provee un verbo plural en el futuro que no califica. Y la respuesta (D) es verbo singular y no califica.

90. La respuesta correcta es A.
La oración necesita un sustantivo plural y la respuesta (A) lo provee. Según el tema del texto, la respuesta (B) no califica. Según el tema del texto, la respuesta (C) no califica. La respuesta (D) no califica tampoco porque es sustantivo singular.

91. La respuesta correcta es B.
La oración necesita un artículo masculino plural, y la respuesta (B) lo provee. La respuesta (A) no califica porque es artículo femenino singular, la respuesta (C) es artículo singular masculino, y la respuesta (D) no califica porque es pronombre masculino singular, y la respuesta.

Archivo Municipal de Saltillo. (1886). Infolios de la Gazeta del Saltillo, Reglas para la vida (airada). Source: http://www.archivomunicipaldesaltillo.info

92.   ¿Qué acción realiza la mujer?

   A.   Tejer.

   B.   Coser.

   C.   Cocer.

   D.   Comer.

La respuesta correcta es la B.

La razón es porque la mujer tiene aguja e hilo—ella cose a mano. No tiene dos agujas grandes para indicar que está tejiendo, así que la respuesta (A) no es correcta. La mujer no está metiendo o sacando algún artículo de comida del horno, así que no está cociendo y la respuesta (C) no es correcta. La mujer no está comiendo y la respuesta (D) no es correcta tampoco.

Novo, S. (2014). Estrenadores vs conservadores. [Newspaper]. Source:

93.   ¿Qué se observa en la imagen?

    A.   Sombreros.

    B.   Carrera de caballos.

    C.   Artículos antiguos.

    D.   Un piano.

La respuesta correcta es C.
Según la imagen, la respuesta más completa es (C) porque se observa una colección de artículos antiguos. Aunque se ven algunos sombreros, no se ven solamente y por esa razón la respuesta (A) no es correcta. No se ve una carrera de caballos, y por esa razón la respuesta (B) no es correcta. Aunque se ve un piano, no es el único artículo observado y por esa razón, (D) no es la respuesta más mejor.

Limón, N. (2014). Estrategias de autorrepresentación fotográfica, el caso de Frida Kahlo. UC3M

94. ¿Qué trae puesto el sujeto?

    A. Pantalones.

    B. Un abrigo.

    C. Una falda.

    D. Un tutú.

La respuesta correcta es C.
El sujeto (la mujer) no trae pantalones y por esa razón, la respuesta (A) no es correcta. La mujer no trae abrigo y por eso la respuesta (B) no es correcta. Y la mujer (el sujeto) trae falda larga-no falda corta (o tutú) y por esa razón la respuesta (D) no es la respuesta más mejor.

Vanguardia Liberal. (2015). Tom Cruise recorre el país visitando las locaciones de su película "mena". [Newspaper]. Source: http://www.vanguardia.com

95.   ¿De qué se trata la noticia?

A.   De una invitación a una película.

B.   Del rodaje de una película.

C.   Del estreno de una película

D.   De la visita a las locaciones de una película.

La respuesta correcta es D.

Según el texto de la noticia, se trata de la visita a las locaciones de una película, y la respuesta (D) es correcta. No se trata de una invitación a una película, así que la respuesta (A) no es correcta. No se trata del rodaje de una película, y por eso la respuesta (B) no es correcta. También no se trata del estreno de una película y por esa razón, la respuesta (C) no es correcta.

96.   ¿Cuántos días durará la visita?

    A.   Una quincena.

    B.   Hasta enero de 2017.

    C.   Nueve días.

    D.   Nueve semanas.

La respuesta correcta es C.
Según la noticia, la visita durará nueve (9) días, y la respuesta (C) es correcta. La visita no durará una quincena y por esa razón la respuesta (A) no es correcta. La visita no durará hasta enero de 2017 y por esa razón, la respuesta (B) no es correcta. Y la visita no durará nueve semanas y por esa razón, la respuesta (D) no es correcta.

Ana es deportista y social. Mónica es callada y prefiere leer un buen libro durante su tiempo libre. Rocío es nadadora y también forma parte del equipo de básquetbol. María quiere ser actriz y bailarina profesional. Karla disfruta escribir poemas y pasar tiempo en la biblioteca.

97.   **De acuerdo con el párrafo, ¿quiénes podrían llegar a ser mejores amigas en base de sus intereses?**

    A.   Mónica y Rocío

    B.   Rocío y Ana.

    C.   Mónica y María.

    D.   Karla y María.

La respuesta correcta es B.
La razón es porque Rocío y Ana comparten un interés en los deportes.

La llamativa anémona de mar debe su nombre a la flor anémona. Esta última forma es parte de una familia de 120 especies con formas y colores variados. Procede del Japón y es utilizada comúnmente para el diseño de jardines, las cuales brotan en la primavera.

98.   ¿De qué se trata el párrafo?

    A.   De las anémonas de mar.

    B.   De las anémonas de luz.

    C.   De las flores anémona.

    D.   De las anémonas del Japón.

La respuesta correcta es C.
Según el tema del texto, aunque las anémonas del mar son mencionadas, el texto no se trata solamente de ellas, y por esa razón la respuesta (A) no es correcta. Las anémonas de luz no son mencionadas y por eso la respuesta (B) no es correcta. Aunque se menciona que las anémonas proceden de Japón, eso no es el único tema del texto, y por eso la respuesta (D) no es correcta.

La pólvora negra es la mezcla explosiva más antigua, obtenida a base de tres sustancias que por separado están exentas de daño--azufre, carbón vegetal, y salitre. La fecha y circunstancias de su descubrimiento son inciertas todavía. Conocida desde el Siglo XIII, se utilizó para sustituir a los sistemas de propulsión de armas.

99.   ¿Cuál debería ser el título del párrafo?

    A.   *La historia de la pólvora negra.*

    B.   *Cómo hacer pólvora negra.*

    C.   *Los ingredientes de la pólvora negra.*

    D.   *La pólvora negra y sus usos.*

La respuesta correcta es A.
Según el tema del texto y el contenido, la respuesta más mejor es la (A).

Albert Einstein no pronunció alguna palabra hasta los dos años de edad. Cuando al fin habló, todo lo repetía dos veces. La mayor parte de su infancia la pasaba solo, jugando principalmente con juguetes mecánicos. En contra de lo que se cree, Einstein no fue un mal estudiante. Al llegar a la edad adulta, era tanta su fama que sólo se rodeaba de celebridades y personas importantes. Se cuenta que en una ocasión Marilyn Monroe le hizo una propuesta ciertamente peculiar, diciéndole que si ellos dos tuvieran hijos y heredaban su genio y la belleza de ella, serían gran personas. A lo que Einstein respondió, «Pero imagínate si ellos heredaran mi belleza y tu inteligencia, nadie los quisiera».

100. ¿Qué mito se desmiente en el párrafo?

    A. Que Einstein era un mal estudiante.

    B. Que Einstein habló hasta ya muy tarde en su vida.

    C. Que Einstein era soltero.

    D. Que Marilyn Monroe le propuso matrimonio.

La respuesta correcta es A.

Según la información en las líneas 3 y 4 del texto, la respuesta correcta es la (A).

Cuando hablamos de los objetos, pensamos también en su utilización en los diferentes espacios de la casa, por ejemplo el espacio social, el íntimo y el de los servicios. También la evolución de esos objetos refleja las influencias culturales sucesivas que ha tenido la región. Primero tenemos la entrada de la casa. Antiguamente las ciudades novohispanas no estaban pavimentadas. Había lodo y estiércol en las calles. Antes de pasar al interior había tapetes para que el visitante pudiera quitarse el polvo de los zapatos. Después se le invitaba a pasar.

101.   ¿Cuál de las siguientes opciones sustituye la palabra «sucesivas» en la tercera línea?

A.   Siguientes.

B.   Repetidas.

C.   Progresivas.

D.   Continuas.

La respuesta correcta es D.

Según la información en la tercera línea del texto, la respuesta correcta es la (D).

En el año 3000 antes de Cristo, los chinos descubrieron que los filamentos que cubrían los capullos de los gusanos de seda podían ser tratados y convertidos en tejido. China guardó el secreto de la sericultura hasta el año 300 antes de Cristo. Más tarde, el secreto llegó hasta Corea debido a los tejedores coreanos que trabajaban en China. Japón aprendió a desarrollar la técnica pronto.

Los comerciantes fueron quienes llevaron la seda hasta Europa a través de la ruta de 4,000 millas bautizada como la «Ruta de la Seda».

En Roma, la ley prohibía a los hombres llevar seda porque la consideraban algo demasiado femenino.

Dos monjes persas llevaron gusanos de seda de contrabando hasta Constantinopla en el Siglo VI, y así llegó el arte de la producción de seda hasta Europa, donde floreció hasta la Segunda Guerra Mundial.
La seda sigue siendo un producto de lujo y alto estatus.

102. **Sinónimo de la palabra «tratados» en la línea 2:**

   A.   Convenios.

   B.   Acuerdos.

   C.   Procesos.

   D.   Negociar.

La respuesta correcta es C.
Según el tema de la oración, la respuesta correcta es la (C).

103. **¿Cómo fue que el arte de la producción de seda llegó a Europa?**

   A.   De contrabando.

   B.   Por los comerciantes.

   C.   Por la «Ruta de la Seda».

   D.   Debido a la Segunda Guerra Mundial.

La respuesta correcta es A.
Según la información en la línea diez (10) del texto la respuesta correcta es la (A).

104. **¿Cuál debería ser el título del párrafo?**

   A.   China y los gusanos de seda.

   B.   La seda en China.

   C.   Los contrabandistas persas.

   D.   La ley de seda en Roma.

La respuesta correcta es B.
Según el tema del texto, la respuesta correcta es la (B).

Las lenguas diversas se extinguen con rapidez. De las 7,000 que existen hoy, sólo se hablarán la mitad al finalizar el Siglo XXI. Lenguas como el Uranino; hablado por apenas 3,000 personas en el Amazonas, el Halkomelem; hablado por doscientos en La Canadá y el Tofa; hablado por no más de personas en Siberia, se enfrentan a un futuro incierto.

Los parlantes nativos dejan de utilizar sus lenguas maternas por varios motivos. Tal vez empezaron a utilizar lenguas más dominantes, con más prestigio o más conocidas. Motivados probablemente por las políticas oficiales del Estado para suprimir el idioma o por presión social. Actualmente se fuerza a los niños de todo el mundo para que aprendan las lenguas que predominan hoy día en el planeta.

Cuando una lengua muere, se lleva con ella muchas otras cosas, tal como conocimientos únicos acerca del planeta y sus criaturas, un tesoro de mitos y poesía, y una ventana que nos puede ayudar a descifrar el funcionamiento de la mente humana. Los conservacionistas de lenguas trabajan para revivir las lenguas muertas que aún pueden salvarse y documentar aquellas cuya salvación es imposible antes de que desaparezcan para siempre.

National Geographic, 2015

105. **¿Qué tipo de texto es?**

    A. Informativo.

    B. Satírico.

    C. Poesía.

    D. Comparativo.

La respuesta correcta es A.
Según el tema del texto, la respuesta correcta es la (A).

106. ¿Qué sucede cuando muere una lengua?

    A. Se lleva la sabiduría de la cultura que la portaba.

    B. Aparecen lenguas estándares nuevas que hablan de criaturas
        diversas.

    C. Es más difícil comprender el funcionamiento de la mente humana.

    D. Hay que documentarla antes de que muera para siempre.

La respuesta correcta es A.
Podríamos argumentar que todas las opciones, excepto el " B " son
correctas . De hecho , A, C y D se producen cuando muere una lengua , pero
lo primero que ocurre es A. C , es una derivación de un suceso . Por lo
tanto , me gustaría seguir con A.

El zar y la camisa

₁Un zar, hallándose enfermo, dijo:
-¡Daré la mitad de mi reino a quien me cure!
*Entonces todos los sabios celebraron una junta para buscar una manera de
curar al zar, mas no encontraron medio alguno.*
Uno de ellos sin embargo, declaró que era posible curar al zar.
*Si sobre la tierra se encuentra un hombre feliz, dijo, quítesele la camisa y
que se la ponga el zar, con lo que éste se curará.*
*El zar hizo buscar en su reino a un hombre feliz. Los enviados del soberano se
esparcieron por todo el reino, mas no pudieron descubrir a un hombre feliz.*
No encontraron un hombre contento con suerte.
*El uno era rico, pero estaba enfermo; el otro gozaba de salud, pero era pobre;
aquél, rico y sano, se quejaba de su mujer; aquel otro hombre, de sus hijos.*
*Todos deseaban algo. Cierta noche, muy tarde, el hijo del zar, al pasar
frente a una pobre choza, oyó que alguien exclamaba:*
Gracias a Dios he trabajado y comido bien. ¿Qué me falta?
*El hijo del zar se sintió lleno de alegría; inmediatamente mandó que le
llevaran la camisa de aquel hombre, a quien en cambio había de darle
cuánto dinero exigiera.*
*Los enviados se presentaron a toda prisa en la casa de aquel hombre para
quitarle la camisa; pero el hombre feliz era tan pobre que no tenía camisa.*
                        ~ León Tolstoi, «El zar y la camisa», 1992

107.   ¿Qué tipo de texto es?

A.   Satírico.

B.   Informativo.

C.   Poema.

D.   Narrativo.

La respuesta correcta es A.
Según el tema del texto, la respuesta correcta es la (A).

108.   ¿Quién se quejaba de sus hijos?

A.   El zar.

B.   El hombre pobre.

C.   El hombre sin camisa

D.   El hombre rico.

La respuesta correcta es B.
Según la información en la línea doce (12) del texto la respuesta correcta es la (B).

109.   ¿Cómo está el hombre más feliz del mundo de acuerdo con la historia?

A.   Pobre.

B.   Rico.

C.   Feliz.

D.   Risueño.

La respuesta correcta es A.
Según el tema del texto, la respuesta correcta es la (A).

110. ¿Quién encontró al hombre más feliz?

A. El zar.

B. Los sabios del zar.

C. El hijo del zar.

D. Los enviados del zar.

La respuesta correcta es C.
Según la información en las líneas 13 y 14 del texto la respuesta correcta es la (C).

111. ¿Quién es el personaje principal?

A. El zar.

B. El hombre sin camisa.

C. El hijo del zar.

D. La camisa.

La respuesta correcta es A.
Según el tema del texto, la respuesta correcta es la (A).

112. ¿Para qué necesitaba el zar una camisa?

A. Porque no tenía una.

B. Porque tenía frío.

C. Para ser feliz.

D. Para curarse.

La respuesta correcta es D.
Según el tema del texto, la respuesta correcta es la (D).

113. ¿Cuál es la moraleja de la historia?

   A. El dinero no compra la felicidad.

   B. Las camisas hacen felices a los hombres.

   C. Los hijos siempre son buenos encontrando lo que se les pida.

   D. Padres e hijos deben pasar más tiempo juntos para lograr la felicidad.

La respuesta correcta es A.
Según el tema del texto, la respuesta correcta es la (A).

Los dioses que adoraban los naturales de esta tierra--la Nueva España
Los aztecas tenían varios dioses que, según sus creencias, intervenían en los asuntos humanos y en algunas ocasiones, hasta los dirigían. Eran dioses celestes y a ellos estaban consagrados los templos.
El dios principal era Huitzilopochtli, el sol, el guerrero eternamente joven, que luchaba contra los demás dioses para que los hombres pudieran vivir. Vencía a la noche y hacía surgir el día nuevo.

El dios de la lluvia, Tláloc, era muy antiguo. Su aparición se remontaba a la época tolteca, 200 A.C. Como tenía el poder sobre la lluvia, a él se le pedía el crecimiento y la vida. En la Tercera Era, Tláloc trajo la luz.

A Quetzalcóatl, la serpiente emplumada, el dios de la sabiduría y del planeta Venus, se le adoraba en distintas configuraciones. Era el señor de la Segunda Era, la de los cuatro vientos, durante la cual el mundo fue devastado por los huracanes y los hombres se convirtieron en monos.

Este dios, llamado Huitzilopochtli, fue robustísimo de grandes fuerzas y muy belicoso-- gran destruidor de pueblos y matador de hombres. En las guerras era como fuego vivo, muy temeroso a sus contrarios y así, la divisa que traía era una cabeza de dragón, que echaba fuego por la boca y era muy espantable. También era ni romántico o embaidor, que se transformaba en figura de aves y bestias diversas.

Este dios, llamado Páinal, era como sota capitán, porque el arribo dicho, como mayor capitán, dictaba cuándo se había de hacer guerra a algunas provincias. Éste, como su vicario, sería para cuando repentinamente se ofrecía salir al encuentro de los enemigos, porque entonces era menester que este Páinal, que quiere decir «ligero», «apresurado», salía en persona a mover a la gente para que con toda prisa salieran a haberse con los enemigos.

El dios llamado Tezcatlipoca era tenido por verdadero dios e invisible, el cual andaba en todo lugar--en el cielo, en la tierra, y en el infierno. Y tenían que, cuando andaba en la tierra, movía guerras, enemistades, y discordias de donde surgían fatigas y desasosiegos.

Decían que él mismo incitaba a unos contra otros para que tuvieran guerras y por esto le llamaban Nécoc Yáotl, que significa «sembrador de discordias de ambas partes». Y decían que sólo él entendía el regimiento del mundo y que sólo él daba las prosperidades y riquezas y que, solamente él, las quitaba cuando se le antojaba. Daba riquezas, prosperidades y fama y fortaleza y señoríos y dignidades y honras y las quitaba cuando se le antojaba.

Este dios Tláloc Tlamacazqui, era el dios de las lluvias. Lo tenían por el que daba las lluvias para que se regaran las tierras, mediante la cual se criaban todas las hierbas, árboles, frutas, y mantenimientos. También le tenían por el que enviaba el granizo, los relámpagos, y los rayos, las tempestades del agua así como los peligros de los ríos y del mar.

El nombre, Tláloc Tlamacazqui quiere decir que es dios que habita en el paraíso terrenal y que otorga a los hombres lo necesario para el mantenimiento de la vida corporal.

~ **Fray Bernardino de Sahagún, Narraciones Históricas, 1590.**

114.   ¿Cuál es el tema principal del texto?

A.   La religión Azteca.

B.   Las memorias de Fray Bernardino de Sahagún.

C.   Huitzilopochtli.

D.   Tláloc Tlamacazqui.

La respuesta correcta es A.
Según el tema del texto, la respuesta correcta es la (A).

115.   **¿Cuál pudiera ser un título alterno al actual?**

A.   *Las aventuras de los Dioses en la Nueva España.*

B.   *Los poderes de los Dioses Divinos.*

C.   *Los Dioses del Olimpo en la Nueva España.*

D.   *Los Dioses Aztecas y sus encomiendas respectivas.*

La respuesta correcta es D.
Según el tema del texto, la respuesta correcta es la (D).

116.   **¿Qué tipo de texto es?**

A.   Texto informativo.

B.   Texto literario.

C.   Texto histórico.

D.   Texto narrativo.

La respuesta correcta es C.
Según el tema del texto, la respuesta correcta es la (C).

117.   **¿A qué se refiere la frase «a haberse» en la línea 23?**

A.   A encontrarse.

B.   A verse.

C.   A tenerse.

D.   A buscarse.

La respuesta correcta es A.
Según el tema de la oración, la respuesta correcta es la (A).

118. ¿Qué error de redacción se observa en la línea 33?

    A. No hay concordancia en el texto.

    B. La palabra, «fortaleza» se escribe con «s», «fortalesa»

    C. Se repite la letra «y».

    D. Faltan comas.

La respuesta correcta es C.
Según la información en la línea 33 del texto la respuesta correcta es la (C).

119. ¿A qué se refiere la frase, «se criaban todas las hierbas»" en la línea 36?

    A. Había que educar a las hierbas.

    B. Las hierbas eran cultivadas.

    C. Había que podar las hierbas.

    D. Todas las hierbas crecían por doquier.

La respuesta correcta es B.
Según la información en la línea 36 del texto la respuesta correcta es la (B).

120. ¿Cuál de los dioses era grande físicamente?

    A. Tláloc Tlamacazqui.

    B. Huitzilopochtli.

    C. Quetzalcóatl.

    D. Páinal.

La respuesta correcta es B.
Según la información en el primer y cuarto párrafo del texto la respuesta correcta es la (B).

XAMonline
The CLEP Specialist

Individual Sample Tests in ebook format with full explanations

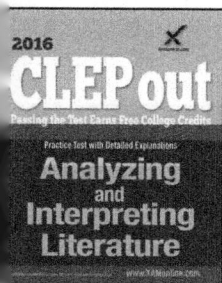

eBooks

All 33 CLEP sample tests are available as ebook downloads from retail websites such as **Amazon.com** and **Barnesandnoble.com**

American Government	9781607875130
American Literature	9781607875079
Analyzing and Interpreting Literature	9781607875086
Biology	9781607875222
Calculus	9781607875376
Chemistry	9781607875239
College Algebra	9781607875215
College Composition	9781607875109
College Composition Modular	9781607875437
College Mathematics	9781607875246
English Literature	9781607875093
Financial Accounting	9781607875383
French	9781607875123
German	9781607875369
History of the United States I	9781607875178
History of the United States II	9781607875185
Human Growth and Development	9781607875444
Humanities	9781607875147
Information Systems	9781607875390
Introduction to Educational Psychology	9781607875451
Introductory Business Law	9781607875420
Introductory Psychology	9781607875154
Introductory Sociology	9781607875352
Natural Sciences	9781607875253
Precalculus	9781607875345
Principles of Macroeconomics	9781607875406
Principles of Microeconomics	9781607875468
Principles of Marketing	9781607875475
Principles of Management	9781607875468
Social Sciences and History	9781607875161
Spanish	9781607875116
Western Civilization I	9781607875192
Western Civilization II	9781607875208

TO ORDER Individual full length sample test are available online **amazon** or **BARNES&NOBLE** BOOKSELLERS

XAMonline

CLEP

Full Guides

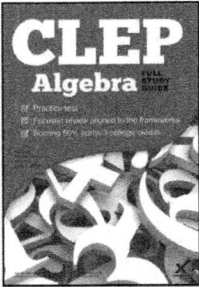

CLEP College Algebra
ISBN: 9781607875307
Price: $34.99

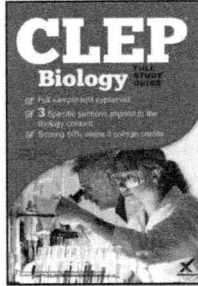

CLEP Biology
ISBN: 9781607875314
Price: $34.99

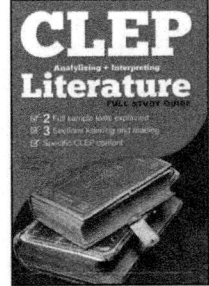

CLEP Analyzing and
Interpreting Literature
ISBN: 978160787526
Price: $34.99

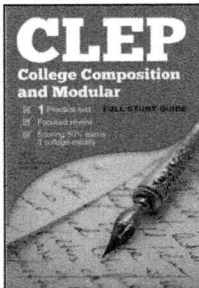

CLEP College Composition
and Modular
ISBN: 9781607875277
Price: $14.99

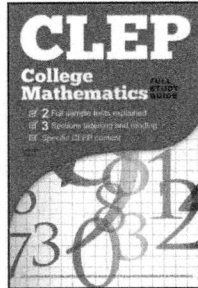

CLEP College Mathematics
ISBN: 9781607875321
Price: $34.99

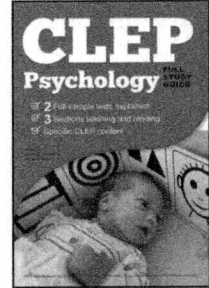

CLEP Psychology
ISBN: 978160787525
Price: $34.99

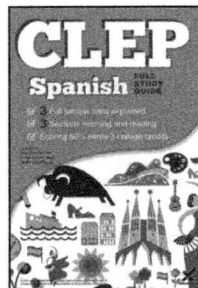

CLEP Spanish
ISBN: 9781607875284
Price: $34.99

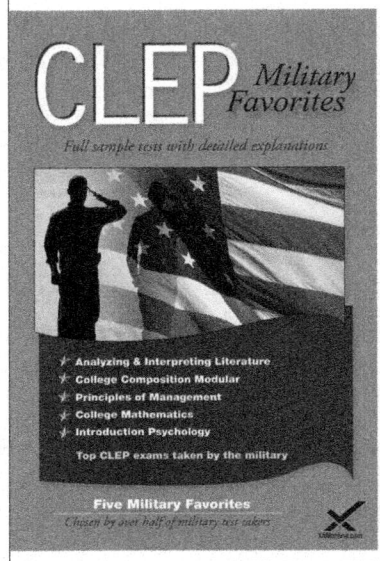

CPSIA information can be obtained
at www.ICGtesting.com
Printed in the USA
BVOW06s0240120917
494630BV00010B/74/P

9 781607 875765